What Deepest Remains

the journey home

A novel by

Joseph Andrew Holsworth

LeRue Press, LLC
Lrpnv.com

Books by LeRue Press may be purchased for educational, business or sales promotional use. To order additional copies contact:

LeRue Press
280 Greg St. #10
Reno, NV 89502.
www.lrpnv.com

Author Photo: Shannon Balazs

Hardcover
ISBN: 978-1-938814-27-3

Paperback
ISBN: 978-1-938814-86-0

Library of Congress Control Number: 2018962312

First Edition

10 9 8 7 6 5 4 3 2 1

Arous'd and angry, I'd thought to beat the alarum, and urge relentless war,
But soon my fingers fail'd me, my face droop'd and I resign'd myself,
To sit by the wounded and soothe them, or silently watch the dead;)
Years hence of these scenes, of these furious passions, these chances,
Of unsurpass'd heroes, (was one side so brave? the other was equally brave;)
Now be witness again, paint the mightiest armies of earth,
Of those armies so rapid so wondrous what saw you to tell us?
What stays with you latest and deepest? of curious panics,
Of hard-fought engagements or sieges tremendous what deepest remains?

-From Walt Whitman's "The Wound-Dresser"

DEDICATION

This book was written for Paige Pulley

ACKNOWLEDGEMENTS

Special thanks to Kay Sue Holsworth, Skip Holsworth, Bob Benski, Tom Barbash, Oliver X, Janice Hermsen, Barry Peterson, Jennifer Ring, Lauren Castro, Ben Castro, Nathan Singley, Armando Ruiz, Kristina Cann, Cody Cann, Lee Cagle, Robert Brown, Joseph Cruz, and Tracy Tucker.

What
Deepest
Remains

CHAPTER ONE
Ramadi

EVERYTHING SMELLED LIKE FRESH bread and hot tea. I had been in war before. I had seen combat in four different countries. The city was much larger before the fighting. It was still bigger than most of our towns back home in the States. A very large and picturesque Mosque centered the city's square and everything was golden and white. The streets were well paved and the buildings were tall and made of concrete that was painted gray, tan, or brown.

Nothing had ever been like this. The fighting was much harder and lasted longer. The enemy didn't turn and run, even when outgunned. And on our side, we had lost the reserve we once had. The years had been unkind to our cause and even the most vigilant warrior began to contemplate his reason for fighting. But a soldier rarely contemplates his enemy's reasons for fighting. It is not within us to see the plight of our foe, for we have both been cast into the same political arena of stench and death. We are actors on their stage, shrouded with the same treacherous drapery of patriotic sentimentality. In those rare instances when we come face to face with the other side, we see that our enemy lives and breathes as we do. And after, when we go back to killing each other, we are no longer patriotic or brave. We are then savage and weak.

My team had taken fire each of the last twenty-three days and it showed in both our attitude and expression. Our battalion had already suffered great casualties. I had been luckier than most sergeants and not lost any of my men yet. We had killed many enemy fighters. We had been in country for over four months and were increasingly hostile to enemy and civilian alike. By this time, I knew only one thing about war: today's soldier needn't dishonor himself to come home in shame.

The sky was most beautiful in the early mornings and I tried to see it every day. Dawn's break was somehow much slower than it is in the west. The dark orange sun emerges like a low-lit bulb, creeping only slightly over the distanced horizon. It peaks over the swirling dust like a dragging minute hand. From all directions the chilling echoes of Muslim prayer shouts bombard the senses. The morning air is already warm but soothing compared to the late spring heat. The light winds feel good as they blow over the back of your neck and hit your face at just the right angle, but this was rare.

There was a simplistic beauty in the sparse landscape. The ground lay flat in all directions, so you could see for miles wherever you looked. In the late afternoon, the sun shined through the trees and the swooping swallows were replaced by diving sparrows and singing babblers. Vegetation was light but the trees were full and green and looked much like California palms. The city's allure came from above the streets, trees, and buildings. They had their own kind of air and the sun could not have been the same one that we watched rise from the training grounds of Fort Bragg.

We were in the largest city and the capital of the province. Ramadi was paramount to military operations for not just the war in Iraq, but the entire military operation known colloquially as the "War on Terror". High-ranking and special operating Mujahedeen and Al Qaeda sects had made a steady home out of the city since early 2004 and were staging both large movement and specialized insurgencies all over the country. What little ground had been made through the Marines' efforts to take control of the city the year before had been since lost by an increasing counter insurgency. The First Battle of Ramadi occurred during the same time as the First Battle of Fallujah. The aftermath of this fighting had misappropriated the military's resources toward Fallujah and set the stage for our grim six-week stay in Ramadi. We were pushing toward summer and each day grew hotter. Casualties were high on both sides.

Thoughts of our dead brothers weighed on both mind and trigger finger. Much of the fighting had moved to the city's streets and into the homes. It was my team's fifth week in Ramadi and the rest of our platoon had just met up with us from running operations in the town of Haditha. My team was the only one in the convoy who had been to where we were going. It's probably why we were the only ones not saying anything.

We always hit them at night. It was four hours before daybreak. My team had slept five good hours and had a hot meal. We had time to call home before it started. I went over the topographical maps instead of making a phone call home. It wouldn't have made any difference either way.

The moonlight shined brightly and the sky was clear of any clouds. The bright light from the moon was amplified against the light tan dust of the ancient ground. The sun had gone away long ago and wouldn't be up any time soon but the scene glowed with the dull light of the blue desert moon. We gathered in a semi-circle around the Sergeant Major. He didn't always say anything before we left the wire.

His voice rang boisterously over the anxious ears of seventeen young soldiers, "Welcome to Ramadi paratroopers. This here is the wild west."

A simultaneous roar of *"Hoooah Sergeant Major,"* blew with enough force to knock a lesser man off his feet. He was young for his rank, a man of barely forty. He was tall and broad shouldered, his figure standing before his battalion was akin to that of the Homeric gods. He stood large and fully dressed in his battle uniform and spoke loudly as he held his assault rifle in one arm by his side. His presence was such as to lend his bravery and confidence to anyone within his proximity.

"Make no mistake about it paratroopers, you are now in the most hostile area of operations in this entire goddamn theater of combat."

As he began to speak, conversation halted and feet stopped stirring in the dust below. He took a deep breath and his already enormous chest expanded like a manta ray and he spoke the words of a man who still believed we had a war to win.

"Men *will* die tonight. How many of you and how many of them will depend upon you, paratroopers. Sergeant Hoskins and his team will be leading the convoy. Make sure to check all your batteries before you roll out. And know this, men; you-are-now-in-Ramadi. This is the hottest place on the map," he paused and spit a wad of chewed up tobacco to the ground with the force of a falling mortar round and continued his briefing. "And subsequently, the rules of engagement have changed in this area of operations. We only operate at night in Ramadi and the city's curfew is set at twenty-hundred hours so--a*rmed or unarmed—engage any male you see who looks like he's fourteen years or older. You hear me, men? Kill anybody you see of age, with or without a weapon! Any questions?"*

Silence fell upon us all, '*armed or unarmed?*' I thought to myself, '*fourteen or older?*' There was a strange emphasis in his wording. He continued to roar down at us from above,

"Know the battle plan and listen to your NCOs. May God be with you. Airborne men!"

The horseshoe formation, surrounding him like a pack leader, yelled back in one collective voice of unbridled youth, *"Airborne Sergeant Major!"*

He leaped from atop the truck and his feet hit the ground, sending bits of rock and dust six feet in every direction. I looked up at the stars for a moment and could see thousands, the air was thin and the sky was clear and everybody would see us coming.

The four squads went to their respective trucks. As decided in the op order, my team would be in the lead vehicle per the usual routine. Kratz approached me wearing the same crooked smile he always did. He was a lengthy six feet with buzzed light brown hair. A prominent brow and sharp nose gave a look of authority to his expression that few men twice his age could hold.

He came to America at eight when his parents emigrated from Russia. His father, whom I'd met once, was a hardened ex-Soviet grunt who, like me, skinned his teeth against the Afghanis in his country's own failed occupation of the land. Kratz's English was perfectly audible, but he spoke with a thick accent reminiscent of a couple of the biggest action stars of our generation. His given name was Maksym, which had been predictably shortened to 'Mac'. The name Maksym simply means "the greatest" and for Kratz, it was merely adequate. Were it not for his proficiency as a paratrooper and team leader, many more soldiers, including myself, would be dead.

Mac was drinking Red Bull from the can. The army was re-supplying us with the energy drinks as regularly as toilet paper and MRE's. The thin can rested atop a magazine pouch on his tac-vest. His helmet hung casually from the butt end of his chest slung M-4. Like all of us, his uniform was sterile, meaning we wore no patches or rank identification, standard operating procedure in Ramadi. His uniform was worn, dirty, and stained. We had been running continuous operations and had not been able to wash our clothes in many weeks. None of us thought anything of it by this time, least of all Mac. Accompanying his soldiering skills, Mac carried a confident swagger that I counted on to lend to my increasingly fragile hope that we'd all make it home alive.

"One more, Sergeant." He smiled widely, and I felt better in seeing it.

"Last one, man." I said.

"You nervous?" he asked. Mac must have been, or he wouldn't have asked me. I was nervous too.

"Nah. Same shit."

My words sent his attention to the ground at our feet. Mac drew a line in the dust with his boot.

Nodding in slow agreement, the words fell slowly from his mouth, "Yeah, just one more, Sergeant."

I pulled a can of long cut tobacco from my right cargo pocket and began packing it without the usual vigor of slamming my index finger against side. I gave it two light taps, twisted the top slowly and exposed the moist fragrant leaves. The smell of fresh chewing tobacco was as satisfying to a combat soldier as fresh spring air to a character in a Jane Austin novel. Without him asking, I put the open can in front of Mac's wandering eyes. He pulled one glove off and took a quarter of the can in one big pinch.

"I'm gonna check the boys, make sure the fill on the radio is good. And check for an extra battery in my assault pack too, man," I said.

"Gotcha, Sergeant."

In addition to Mac, I had two other men under my command. They were Private First Class, Horton and Donaldson. Horton was my gunner and had been in the platoon the longer of the two. He was unrivaled in the battalion at running the .50 caliber machine gun and had gotten our team out of a few harry situations with his handy work. Bright-eyed, block headed and short and stout, but quick in both mind and body. Horton's skills and wherewithal as a paratrooper rendered my job much easier than it might have otherwise been.

Donaldson had come to the platoon half-way through the deployment as a replacement for my guy, O'Connor, who took a round through his right ankle two months before. The little I knew of Donaldson was that he was a nineteen-year-old kid from somewhere in Pennsylvania who worked at a pet shop for a year after high school, and now he was the greenest private in all the battalion and *my* responsibility.

For Mac and me both, this was to be the last in a long line of missions we had performed during our tenure with the 82nd Airborne Division. Like an ambitious fool, I had signed up for four years in the infantry instead of the obligatory three. I figured since kids went to college for four years, I'd do my full four as well.

Mac signed up for three and was on his way out with me. In total, this was my one hundred sixty-sixth combat mission. When you have more months in combat than years alive everything turns black. My brow was sweaty even though I felt cold all the way down my back. I tongued the wad of tobacco that sat between my teeth and lip, trying to pack it as tightly as I could. Donaldson or Horton said something to me that I could not hear. It must not have been that important because I don't think they repeated it and I know that Mac went right on without taking notice, I saw as he sat motionless across from me.

Thumbing my M-4 assault rifle, I scraped small collections of dirt from the checkered meshing of the pistol grip with the edge of my nail. I sat staring in the passenger seat of the five ton uparmored Humvee, gazing into what would have been the last barrier a sniper round passed through before it burrowed its way into and through the backside of my unknowing skull. Instead I was looking into a concentrated and well-contained small crack, about the size of a silver dollar. It happened just a couple months prior. The round was stopped by a plate of bulletproof glass, a plate of glass that was not on the Humvees of my first two deployments.

Two months before, we were pulling perimeter security for Alpha Company who was doing a routine patrol outside the city of Haditha, when the bullet fired from a sniper modified AK-47 almost took off my head.

It had been raining for the three days and the dry warmth was a welcomed treat in a place where gifts of circumstance were few and far between. There were four of us in the truck, and I made the casual decision to lower our security to fifty percent, leaving only the turret gunner and myself on high alert. It probably would not have made any difference, given the shot was fired from at least five hundred meters away, but I cannot help but think that had my full attention been on security as it should have been and not split between the MRE lemon poppy-seed pound cake I was enjoying, I would have spotted that sniper. As it was, I was listening to the conversation between Mac and Horton regarding which 1970s celebrity they would most want to have sex with. I remember it vividly, not for the conversation, but for what stopped it.

"Farrah Fawcett, it's easy. No question."

Horton wrinkled his nose in disgust and threw an MRE spoon at Mac.

"Horton, I have four words for you, *Bar-ba-rell-a.*"

"Get the fuck outta here, Mac. Jane Fonda? I knew you was a commie bastard. Hey, Sergeant, you hearin' this shit? Think you outta take Mac's frags and ammo."

Everyone but Donaldson laughed, Horton the loudest, as he was prone to do at his own jokes.

"Who's Jane Fonda?" Donaldson asked.

"Goddamn, Cherry. You really don't know shit about shit, do you?" Horton was the only one in the platoon who still called Donaldson, 'Cherry'.

"What, who is she?" he asked again.

"She's this cunt-rag actress from the 60s and 70s who shot down planes while she was hanging out with an NVA anti-aircraft battalion," Horton answered.

"What? She was an American? An actress?" asked Donaldson.

"Yeah, she's Henry Fonda's daughter, you know, the cowboy."

Donaldson was eating up Horton's fabricated historical account like a freshman sociology major.

"You seen *Easy Rider* at least, right?" I asked.

"Yeah, my dad had it on tape," he answered looking excited that he knew something.

"Yeah, that's Jane Fonda's brother," I said.

"Who, I mean which one, Sergeant?" he asked like he didn't believe me.

"The guy who isn't Dennis Hopper or Jack Nicholson," I said.

"And his sister, Jane, shot down an American plane?" Donaldson asked.

"Well, nah, but she *tried* to," Horton answered.

"But why would she…"

Mac yelled, *"Holy fuck Sergeant! What the fuck was that?"*

"Gun it, Mac. Move!" I yelled back. Before the words were out of my mouth we were already on the move, the spinning tires sending dust and sand in a furious whirlwind of panic. It sounded like an aluminum baseball bat slamming into a cement wall. It took a half second to register. I looked at the black smoking smudge left on the windshield and realized that a sniper had almost taken my head off.

It happened over two months before and had been outweighed by so much that it was no longer even talked about. But I looked at it every time I got in our truck. While I stared down the road and looked around for IED's and triggermen, it was always through that obstructive mark that was a constant reminder of what could have been. It was just a small little grayish speck and crack, but it was so hard to see past.

Our battalion had become more reactionary as the tour progressed. Justified or not, increasing hostilities had changed the rules of the game and now teenagers were on our hit list as well. Just days before a gunner from another squad killed a twelve-year-old on a bicycle for riding too close to the convoy and was later commended for his 'combat readiness.'

"Hey, guys, listen up. I don't give a fuck what the Sergeant Major says about the rules of engagement. Don't just be opening up on any motherfucker walking down the street. There's gonna be all kinds of testosterone flying around tonight, don't pointlessly add to the confusion out there." Mac put on his helmet and quietly added, "We're not here to terrorize these people."

I looked over at him. His eyes peered forward. Without moving his head even slightly, he brought the hand mic to his mouth and said with gravel in his voice, "Blue Devil 7, this is Delta 1 Alpha, radio check over."

"Delta 1 Alpha, this is Blue Devil 7, good copy over."

CHAPTER TWO
Once More Unto the Breach

BEFORE LEAVING THE WIRE, time slows to a drag. Sensations are all heightened save for hearing which goes almost muted. The skin reacts to the slightest touch of wind or grain of sand. The back of my neck was hot; the heat vortexed up through my collar. The inside of my tac- vest was like a swamp. The tobacco in my lip was making my mouth dry, so I spit it out and finished what was left of my Red Bull. Looking down at the tan line on my finger where until just days before my wedding ring had been, I rubbed the skin as if the mark were just a clean spot on my dirty hand. It happened over the phone, but it really happened months, and probably even years before.

We'd almost divorced after my second tour, but the news of my third brought us together before it could all be finalized. I guess she'd had enough time away from me this time to decide that's the way she liked it. She told me that she still loved me but things were just too hard. I knew what she meant even though I said I didn't. She must have known what it was going to be like long before I did. She must have known that me coming home didn't mean that my war would be ending. Our love had faded to the point of only showing itself on those rare instances when we forgot all the ways we'd made each other feel over the years, and we could be those lustful teenagers that were once so enamored with one another's bodies. None of it was real anymore and hadn't been for years, but I hoped it wasn't why she left. Radio interference prevented me from indulging too far into thoughts that served no purpose.

The radio was buzzing and Mac went about like he didn't notice it and maybe didn't. I keyed the hand mic once and the radio fell silent and Mac looked over at me and blinked both eyes with an exaggerated smile and took a magazine from his ammo pouch and set it on the dashboard and said, "Just one more, Sergeant."

"We got this man. It's nothing," I said back with an aim at convincing myself as much as anybody else.

Horton yelled down from the turret, "Fuck yeah we do, Sergeant. We ain't gonna get it on our last goddamn mission."

"No shit, right?" I said. But I knew it didn't make a difference. We could die on that night as easily as any other.

"Hey Drew," Mac said.

"What's up?" I answered. He stopped for a moment like he was going to say never mind.

"What do you think you'll do after all this?" he asked.

"I don't know man, travel a bit. See Paris; maybe Milan. Find a good woman. I'd like a good woman. What do you think you'll do, man?"

"I don't know; never mind."

He cracked his neck to each side and I could tell that Mac's world was different than mine. The one he created for himself that is. All soldiers in war create a different world, one away from all the fighting. Some are filled with drunk college girls and kegged beer. Some are filled with deep sea fishing trips or African safaris, but they all had one thing in common: they all placed the protagonist in the middle of the kind of complete subliminal restitution that only exists in the fantasies of the utterly doomed.

Mac spewed tobacco spit out the window with a reserved fury and wiped the dribblings from his chin with his rolled sleeve and said, "Alright, let's do this. *Last-fucking-one*, Sergeant." He cracked his neck to the other side and hit his fist against the side of his helmet and took a deep breath and held it in deep before letting it out in an abrupt sigh that sounded almost like a cough.

It was time to move out. I put my head out of the still open window. I looked behind at our other three vehicles. The LT, right behind us, gave me a nod with canted eyes and a single motion wave while spitting tobacco out his window. We exchanged uneasy glances and turned on our engines. There was a difference of opinion and an ensuing argument that took place in the operation order before the Sergeant Major's Lombardi speech. The LT, who had just come into Ramadi for this mission, was accustomed to always commanding the lead vehicle and subsequently assumed that he would be commanding my truck.

With little hesitation but with my most polite military tone, I interrupted the LT's request and simply said, "Sir, with respect, you just got to Ramadi two hours ago. You have never been here or taken any of the routes that we are about to go on. I've run over thirty patrols and missions here. My men and I know this area of operations like it was St. Marie Aglese drop zone at Fort Bragg. I need to be in the front of the convoy with my men. And besides, Sir, nobody is leading my team outside this wire but me." From what little I knew of him from before the deployment, he was a good platoon leader and a considerably mild-mannered officer.

"Sergeant, this is my call, not yours. I appreciate your position, but I--"

"Sir, let me stop you right there."

Everybody fell immediately silent as the Sergeant Major spoke, he still had three 7.62 rounds in his back where a Panamanian placed them seventeen years earlier. He spoke softly but assertively. He didn't need to grumble or to growl, he simply spoke, and everybody listened.

"Sergeant Hoskins will be commanding the lead vehicle with his squad."

That was it. There was no explanation, nor argument.

When the Sergeant Major would turn away from the leadership, pointing to something on the topographical map, the LT's eyes would shift over to me. Not one of his glares escaped my notice, I watched him too. The LT was a good man from what I had heard, but I'd heard a lot of things in my time in combat and I believed only what I witnessed myself under fire.

Beyond the many questions regarding our presence in Ramadi as part of a supposed global campaign to rid the world terrorism, I found even our immediate situation to be tactically questionable at best. We had taken fire every time we had taken this route. It was among the most IED prone in the entire theater of combat. My squad had personally been hit by an IED on the same route earlier in the month. And there was no tactical advantage of having our gun trucks going this way. A call came over the radio.

"Delta 1 Alpha. You awake up there? Let's roll out."

"Roger. Just giving anybody who's listening one last minute to think about this."

Mac swung his head toward me but didn't say anything. I smiled at him and didn't want him to think I was serious even though I was. I gave a playful wave out the window to the rest of the convoy and closed the bulletproof glass window behind me. I put in a fresh pinch of tobacco and handed it over to Mac.

I yelled up toward the turret, "Yo Horton, you doing okay up there, man? You see everything alright?"

"All good, Sergeant, good visibility tonight," he yelled back with a disturbingly excited voice.

"Good shit; just stay alert, Horton."

But it wasn't good shit. Good visibility meant only one thing: we made clearer targets for the enemy. At this stage in my military career, my focus had shifted completely away from mission success. I cared only for the safety of my men. My twenty-two months in combat had taught me that at the end of the day it didn't matter how many enemy combatants we killed or captured, the war would continue just the same. The only thing that changed were the soldiers who died.

As we drove through the gates of Ramadi, I had only one thought on my mind, the same thought I'm sure that was on the minds of the rest of my men. I replayed over and over in my head the sequence of events that led up to our second encounter with an IED. It was only slightly more damaging than our first, which is to say that still nobody was injured, our vehicle was not disabled, and we continued about our mission as if nothing had really happened.

The last one, however, differed from the first. It was a direct hit to our vehicle. We were lucky. The device was shoddy and the amount of composition was insufficient to disable our vehicle or kill any of us. But we all felt the blast. The pressure is overwhelming. It feels like you're getting hit by a jet engine from every angle, and all noise is displaced by a hard ringing that feels like a hundred bees are loose in your shaking skull. It was a new kind of war. In the beginning, both sides were just learning; by this time, the books had been written.

We were young but seasoned fighters. Mac and I were the oldest at twenty-two. He came in a year after me. We worked together in Iraq in '04 when I was still a specialist and he was a private. Horton was young but had taken full advantage of every opportunity in proving his proficiency in the gunner's turret. Donaldson was my only wild card. He had done plenty of patrols with us and I knew he could maneuver, but I didn't know if he could kill yet, and moreover, I knew that *he* didn't know yet either.

The mission was simple, especially for my section whose objective was to provide perimeter security for our dismounted Alpha troops that were to be both dropped and picked up by Black Hawk helicopters. The destination was about ten miles away and, given the urban landscape, would take about twenty minutes to travel. Our stated objective was to blockade the two major entrance/exit points to the village with our remaining gun trucks. The Alpha Company dismounts were to be in and out in under two hours.

Visibility was as clear as can be at that hour. The near fullness of the waxing moon and the thickly starred sky made night vision almost unnecessary.

"How you doing over there, Mac?" I asked.

"Look at that fucking moonlight, Sergeant. Fucking Donaldson could drive on a night like this."

Both of his hands gripping the wheel like it was a life he was trying to extinguish told me that his casual demeanor was, as mine was, all show.

He yelled up toward the turret, "Horton, you good up there, man?"

"Good, Mac."

Mac's ability as a leader was not exercised to its fullest potential as a Specialist, but he was satisfied with his rank and position, and wanted nothing else but to do his short time honorably and return home in one piece with dignity. The very nature of war had already rendered this partly impossible for us both. By this time, we were focused on just getting home in one piece.

What came next was what I think about most still. Many years later, the scene repeats itself in my mind like an infinitely repeating 8mm projector in the bowels of hell. I feel it now. It is always with me. Around me. It creeps up my spine and cannot be itched away. It covers me and crushes me still, and I know it will always be there and I would be even more afraid if it someday wasn't.

The noise displacement was like something I had never heard or felt. The blast made a tremendous roar, dull and low in frequency but so loud as to push out all other sound and make your head feel like you were three hundred feet below the sea. My ears didn't ring; rather were just numb to surrounding sound. I felt sick with a thousand punches and although I knew exactly what had just happened, I was confused as to what to do next.

The contents of my mind's wanderings in those short couple of seconds after the blast told me I was still alive and as I looked over at Mac I could see that he was too. He was still driving, looking quickly over at me and then back at the road. His wide-open mouth, crunched brow line, and spinning tongue told me he was trying with everything he had to say something, but I heard nothing. I knew that the blast had come from our rear because there was nothing obstructing us to the front. From the rigor of the impact the blast had likely divided us from the rest of the convoy. I turned around in my seat and could see that Donaldson was at least semi-conscious. There was no visible damage to the interior of the Humvee and I knew immediately that the blast had not penetrated the armor. Fearing what had happened to my half-exposed gunner, I grabbed the loose material of Horton's cargo pants and pulled him into the humvee. I was confused at first at the resistance and still could not hear anything. I tried pulling even harder but could not see what was keeping me from getting Horton into safety, until his knee connected with the side of my helmet sending me back to my seat. Realizing that Horton was at least well enough to be returning machine gun fire at an enemy that the rest of us could not yet see, I grabbed again with only one hand and held onto his pants like he was my child.

Mac pulled me by the inside of my vest to get my attention. Just as my hearing came back to me, I felt the rear of our forty mph accelerating Humvee lift from the ground as if we were about to take flight. Our truck rolled several times.

Fortunately, I had maintained the parental grip on Horton's cargo pants and a combination of the initial blast and Mac's pulling on my vest had jerked Horton down into the turret in what must have been the last possibility to do so. The second blast felt like an eternity after the report of the first, but was actually a matter of seconds. The road was narrow and had old crumbled asphalt paving its route. There was room for two vehicles as long as neither of them was the width of a humvee. Our vehicle lay on its side almost perfectly perpendicular with the road. There was no space on either side of our truck for another vehicle to pass.

My wits were absent, but the blast didn't knock me out. I vividly remember a hard, dull thumping sound that got progressively louder and was accompanied with the addition of guttural heaves after the first few.

"Sergeant. Sergeant. *Sergeant! Sergeant!*" I couldn't make out the words, but knew from the direction of the sound that it was coming directly from my rear and that meant that Donaldson was alive. It took a moment for my mind to return, and once my eyes stopped shaking and my ears released, I too noticed that my confused equilibrium had more than just the nasty blast to account for it. The great acceleration of our Humvee in perfect combination with the IED explosion had sent our vehicle, that now laid on its passenger side, rolling over numerous times until it came to a screeching halt, leaving a trace of sparks that must have looked like July 4th fireworks dancing along our destructed path. Our ears rang like broken alarm clocks and even yelling at the top of our lungs from just feet away, we could scarcely hear each others' words.

"*Donaldson. Don. You okay?*" I yelled.

"*Yeah, I'm okay Sergeant,*" he answered.

I yelled to my turret gunner, "*Horton, Horton!*" My leg was caught between the seat and the door, wedged impossibly from the knee down. I could not turn to see in the back and didn't hear an answer.

"*Where's Horton?*" I yelled.

"*We got him, Sergeant. He's right here!*" Donaldson yelled back.

"*Horton! Horton, you okay?*" I yelled.

Horton didn't answer directly, but his shouts shook the entire truck.

"*Fuck you! Fuck you! You hear me? I'm still alive motherfuckers!*"

He was yelling at the top of his lungs at an enemy that none of us could see. I at least knew he was still combat effective.

"*Horton, you hit?*" I yelled back.

He put his hand on top of his helmet and shook it around and pounded the chest plate of his tac-vest and yelled back, "*Got some cuts on my face, but I ain't bleedin' bad, Sergeant. I'm fine.*"

I yelled toward Mac, "*Mac!*" He was already getting himself unwedged and making his way to the turret.

"We gotta get outta here, Sergeant. Right now," he said back right away.

"My leg's caught. Try getting out through the turret," I said.

"The hatch is closed. Can't get the fucker open," he said.

"Donaldson, try your door," I said.

"Roger, Sergeant," he answered back.

Donaldson tried, but was much smaller than I was, and likely did not fully interpret the dire importance that one of us in the immediate future get one of those doors open. With the aggressive vigor usually reserved only for the three-month sex-starved infantry recruit, I violently ripped my leg free and, pushed open the two hundred fifty -pound door; creating an escape from our ambush vulnerable position. I remember pushing through that door not as a leader or even a soldier, but only a scared and desperate human being. I knew, because I'd put so many combatants in the same spot we were in, right where the dying was sweet.

I unslung my M-4 assault rifle from across my chest and reached outside with it in my hand, placing it on the side of the humvee and pulling myself up and out through the door. I glanced up, only slightly, to see my surroundings. The road was narrow and just up ahead about fifty yards had been blocked off by a series of abandoned and wrecked vehicles. In a quick moment, I thought to myself that even if we had escaped the second blast, we would have been cut off by the blockade in the road. It was frighteningly clear that whoever pulled the trigger on this ambush knew exactly what they were doing. Nothing I had trained for or done in combat prepared me for that desperate situation when all battle tactic goes out the window and you resort back to primal instincts that are inevitably rooted in the hearts of every breathing beast of the Earth.

The buildings were close together and high on both sides. The rooftops were crowded with onlookers or enemies; I didn't know which yet. Brightly lit street lamps, aided by the shining moonlight, provided complete visibility in all direction. To say we were at a disadvantage would be misleading. I was sure that we'd all be dead in minutes. It was the almost complete assurance of our deaths that made it easy to react, nothing mattered anymore.

"Donaldson, forget it. Grab those extra IR chems and get through here," I yelled.

"Mac, here, gimme your weapon. Take my hand." As I lay Mac's M-4 next to mine and pulled him from the humvee, two quick snaps on the pavement followed by a metallic thump to our hood introduced the newest participants into the ambush. We were taking small arms fire from the street, from the building, the rooftops... from God knows where. I knew I wasn't shot, but I could feel a warm wet sensation all down my right leg where it was caught in the seat. My warm blood-soaked pants gave a peculiar contrast to the cool breeze and gunfire passing over my neck.

CHAPTER THREE
Ambush

"WE'RE TAKING FIRE! FUCKING move. Move. Move. Move!"

I was sure that in a matter of seconds our downed vehicle would be struck by a rocket propelled grenade. I hastily grabbed down through the open door, my body laying flush with the side of the vehicle. Mac was the closest and I grasped hold of his forearm, I could feel my fingertips dig into the bulk of his arm like a dull meat hook. He only needed me for an initial boost. I felt the slightest tug on my elbow, and with one swift motion, Mac came elevating up through the open door as if propelled by an additional blast.

"I got him, Sergeant. Here." Mac handed me two smoke grenades from his vest and I picked up my weapon and jumped down off the humvee. Our truck lay almost perfectly perpendicular with the road. The top of the truck now lay facing the direction from which we just came. The two blasts had blown brick, concrete, wood, dirt, dust and metal in all directions. Visibility on the ground was diminished by a whirlwind of gray dust swirling down through the chaos.

Muzzle flashes began coming from the concrete buildings on each side of the road. Crouched to a knee and clinging as closely to the humvee as possible, I concentrated a few shots toward the taller buildings to my left. I deployed the first smoke grenade, throwing it toward the base of the same buildings about one hundred feet in front of me. I did the same with the second grenade on the other side. Only one hundred meters or so to my front on either side of the road were a multitude of open windows and roof top corners that were sporadically illuminated by the muzzle flashes of enemy fighters. They kept popping into windows, firing a few sporadic bursts and disappearing again right when another appeared.

We took cover behind our downed vehicle, although bullets were coming from all directions. I fired single shots into the windows as I saw movement. I did not pick my targets. I did not distinguish my targets in any way. I was frantic and I fired with a desperate necessity to live through what was the most disadvantaged position I had ever been in. In the midst of it all, I forgot about being a team leader and was merely a solider reacting to his team and the enemy in the only way possible to stay alive.

While under heavy fire, a small infantry unit must react to each other's movements with the coordination of Olympic synchronized swimmers while maintaining the improvisational adeptness of a jazz quartet. It was quite literally the fight of our lives. I never expected to make it out, or any of my men. I wanted to kill as many people as possible before I died.

To our front was the blockaded road. Nothing but back alley shanties leading "God knows where" to our sides, I thought scaling the rather pedestrian obstacle seemed the best choice. I had to assume that the blockade was put up to stop our travel up the road in case we got past the blasts of the IED, so I hoped there wasn't anyone waiting on the other side of it. Horton was the next out after Mac. Immediately and without command, he dismounted the top of the vehicle and returned fire toward the side where the smoke was coming. Horton's machine gun fire made an already chaotic scene into a full-fledged shit storm. But that's what combat was: a hot, whirling storm of wet shit. There was no real reason anything happened, to anybody, on either side. Just when you start to make sense of something, the toughest guy in the company gets one leg and both balls blown off by a sack of nails stuffed into a homemade bomb.

Donaldson was last to come down and was quickly right behind Horton. But instead of sliding off the top like his life depended on it as the rest of us did, Donaldson stood straight up and before he could jump down, he was ripped down by a 7.62 mm round that threw him from the top of the humvee like an invisible gladiator. That was it. That was the moment when everything was stripped away from me. I felt a thud to my chest as if I were shot there myself. My armor fell from my shoulders, my helmet from my head, and my rifle from my sweaty palms. My eyes and memory were glued in time to that moment when I was sure that the first of us was dead.

As I came to the other side of the truck, I fired two quick shots up at each side of the road. Then I grabbed for the medical aid bag that was stashed away in Mac's backpack.

I yelled out to Mac and Horton, *"Grab him. Other side of the truck. Let's go!"*

Before I could get to the aid pack, Mac already was flinging Donaldson over his shoulder. He brought him to the other side where Horton took a knee using the front end of the Humvee as cover and he started firing back toward the buildings. I took the rear side and did the same while Mac, who was the best at medical aid, went to work on my young private, a soldier who less than a year ago was selling goldfish to little kids and now was laying shot in some street in Iraq.

Our smoke concealment was non-existent by now and we were taking more and more fire every second. Rounds poured in from both sides of the street. The snapping of near misses told me they were right on us. I was sure that if we didn't get new cover soon, we would all be dead.

"Mac, talk to me. What's going on there? Where's he hit?"

"Hold on!" Mac yelled back.

"I'm fine. Let me up. I'm fine." I could hear Donaldson's shaken voice; he sounded scared, but not faint. I knew it was not mortal.

"I'm fine. It didn't hit me. It went through my assault pack. Let me up." I took a small breath of relief in hearing his voice, but was immediately thrust back into the bleak reality of our fragile situation as the impact of another bullet struck a panel of the Humvee, just inches from my face.

"Check him out, Mac. We gotta move!" I yelled.

"Can you move? Can you move Don; are you alright?" Mac asked.

"Yeah, come on. Let me up," said Donaldson.

Mac yelled toward over the screaming machine gun barrel, "No blood, he isn't bleeding, Sergeant,"

"Then get him up, let's move," I said.

Horton yelled, *"Oh shit, Sergeant. There, to our front, look!"*

Firing one more burst, I looked back over my shoulder and saw lit up by a streetlight in the distance, a group of men mounting a crew served weapon of some kind on top of the blockade of vehicles. The increased fire from our rear in combination with the static muffled screams over the open net of the radio telling anybody who could to push up the road through the ambush, told us that we had nowhere to go but away from the road and through the alley ways.

The alleys were not even wide enough to be described as narrow; they were merely thin. The danger of the alley ways, aside from the obvious complete lack of any kind of maneuverability, was that you were especially susceptible to having homemade explosives or acidic chemicals dropped down onto you from the numerous windows and balconies above. It was hard because you didn't want to ever look up, knowing that whatever was coming would be inevitable, and better to land on one's helmet rather than face. With the machine gun crew ready to cut us to shreds, we had to take it to the alleys and enter the labyrinth.

We all heard the chatter of the eager machine gun crew to our front, I could only imagine their excited anticipation in killing an entire fire team of paratroopers. Few things move a soldier more quickly than the dull metallic slamming of an open bolt feeding the first round of a machine gun pointed at you.

"Through the alleyway. Right now. On me. Move!" I yelled.

We had never been hit so hard, but we all knew that most of the people lingering around after an ambush were either responsible for the explosion or part of a coordinated follow up assault. The first alley we went down was perpendicular with the right side of the road, and from the outside it looked to be the widest. We stacked against the wall, which is to say that we all went to one side of the entrance, in a line, in the same order as we approached. It was not customary for myself, the team leader, to enter first, but given the circumstances, standard operating procedure had taken a back seat to instinct and necessity. I barreled around the corner of the first building, hugging the side so tightly as I came across that I could feel debris coming off as I scraped the rough wall. It was darker than I had thought and I had to put my night optical devices on. Night vision greatly reduced your peripheral sight and depth perception so I only used them if I had to.

I echoed back as I came through, "Clear, I don't see anyone. But put your NODs on. It's too dark."

Mac repeated and sent back, "Put your NODs on. And move out."

We heard M-4 gunfire that had to be coming from the rest of the convoy that was cut off from the blast. Seconds later we heard the unmistakable sound of a MK19 automatic grenade launcher thumping explosive cartridges at two hundred rounds per minute and we knew we still had at least one truck in the fight.

I had no idea where the byzantine path was going to take us, but I was sure that we could not go back on the road. It seemed that we were on the main path through the market area, but there were dozens of smaller outlets jetting off everywhere and in all directions. We couldn't see very far ahead or behind us because every ten paces or so there was another corner. I didn't know what to do next, only that my next few decisions would determine if we lived or died. I turned to see my men's faces. They all looked like boys. I did too; I'm sure of it. I couldn't believe this had happened. Our truck was disabled, we were cut off from the rest of our unit, and it was up to us to get out.

Horton leaned in past Mac and said, "Sergeant, we need to link up with the convoy, yeah?"

I heard him and hesitated slightly before saying, "Yeah, man." I turned to Mac and said, "Yo, Mac, I don't know where any of these goddamn alley ways leads to, man."

Mac looked over his shoulder and said, "Don, keep pointed down there, keep guard on our rear." He stepped up past me and looked down the alley, "Fuuuuck. These mother fuckers twist and fucking zig zag all down around every goddamn bend. Fuck this," he said.

Nobody liked our options. Time to go I decided.

"Alright, Mac, guys, fuck it, I said with a determination that was rooted not in confidence but in nervous haste. "We're just going to follow this main pathway all the way down 'til it leads back to the main road. Then we'll be able to link up with the rest of the convoy." I was just really *hoping* that this was the case but the uncertainty of the battle field must be balanced by a semblance of wherewithal from somebody, and my position on the team dictated that I be the first to attempt the necessary fabrication. "We're gonna take it fast. Stay close, but don't get tripped up. We're gonna double time it, alright? Ready?"

"Wait, Sergeant."

"Donaldson, what?" I growled.

"I can't see shit. Where does this even go?" He asked.

"Don't worry. I got it, just follow Horton, hoooah." I said.

"Let's fuck'n do this, Sergeant." Horton said back.

"Alright, Horton, give that to Don." I pushed a smoke canister into his waiting hand. "Don, pop that smoke. Alright, move." I said.

We moved through as quickly as we could. Every few steps a bending corner, running past one, we took a few quick steps and were at another corner or little offshoot. It felt like being a lab rat in a science experiment, frantically barreling through a maze of mud walls, rock, and concrete. Everywhere above us were dilapidated wooden balconies, some with people; some without. We could hear constant gunfire from the streets, between bursts, screams in both English and Arabic filled the desert night air and it felt like we'd been on the ground for hours.

I stopped short of the road and Mac slammed into me, almost sending me to the ground. He grabbed by tac vest and pulled me back. I looked back and smiled at him and he smiled back at me and for some reason I felt better then. I knew that there was an enemy position close by the distinctive cracking sound of the AK-47; it's a duller and lower sound than our M-4 rifles that fire a smaller round and make more of a snapping sound. If we could get the drop on them, maybe we could turn the tables.

I got on my radio to the commander of the third truck in our convoy, Sgt. Cantrell. "Delta 1, this is Alpha 1, come in over."

There was no response at first and I feared they had been killed.

"Cant! Come in, it's Drew." It was not customary to use names, but call signs felt too impersonal for a time when we could die at any moment.

"I'm here. Hold on." His words were muffled by rifle shots all around. "Drew, Drew, come in." He answered back after a couple seconds.

"I'm here, buddy, over," I said.

"You good, all your guys good? Over."

"We' re good. What's your position? Over." I asked.

"We're set up just down the street, about a hundred meters back from blast. Hold on Drew."

The two-way radio went silent as he released his hand mic, and I imagined Cantrell firing at an opportune target.

He got back on and said, "Drew, you still there? Over."

"I'm here Cant, but we gotta move, we got enemy positions all over us up here." I said.

"Roger. We can't move up the street, they're too dug in. Where are you guys? Over," he said.

"I can hear your guys' MK19, I think we're about two hundred or so meters up the street and around the bend, over."

"Roger. Can your team move through and help us out up there? Over."

"Roger. We'll find a place to come through. I'm going up on the roof, Cant, opposite side of the road. Over."

"Drew, wait. What side of the road are you going to be on? Over."

"I'm on the east side now, we are going to cross over to the west side—break—I'll pop red smoke on the roof so you know where we're at, over."

"Roger. You're going to cross over to the west side of the road, hit the rooftop, and mark your position, three hundred meters up from us. How copy?"

"Roger, Cant, that's a good copy. Alpha 1 out."

"Careful up there, Drew. We got ya back here, man. Delta 1 out."

We prepared to move up and across the road to what looked like a cellar just up the street. The cellar was just the bottom part of a tall three-story building. There were two balconies on the side facing us, but no hostile activity visibly present. We stacked against the right side of the wall in order of our rank.

I knew that Mac was quicker through the door than I was, but also that he would be more selective of his targets than I would be. On one of our first patrols in Ramadi, Mac had done something that I never had, something that he carried with him still and always would.

It was no fault of his own, a tragedy of war without a guilty party, but tell that to the soldier who pulled the trigger. Mac was one of the best I had ever served with, but the accident brought more than scars to his soul, it delivered the slightest hesitancy upon his trigger, one in which we could not afford on that night.

The only way to cross the street was as quickly as possible. Strategy would play little part in the endeavor, timing would be everything and it would be mostly based on luck. We were not only susceptible to enemy fire, but also friendly. I didn't want to give our position away to the enemy by marking our location too early. Crossing the road, I was just as nervous to take a round from one of our guys as I was the enemy. I could have gone over the radio and had them hold their fire for just a few seconds, but I did not want to leave them additionally vulnerable, and honestly, I did not at the time even think of it as a possibility to do so.

I could tell from the sound of the echoing shots bouncing off the buildings that we were still some distance away from the wreckage sight. The narrow alley walls reminded me of moving through the rocky cave dwellings of Eastern Afghanistan. We traded the high desert and mountains for low dessert urban sprawl, but the fighting conditions would overlap in those curious moments in all wars where the stage seems to come together in one collective arena of utter human despondence.

Ready to move, I looked back at Mac and said, "Get off my ass, Mac. Don't bunch up. Be fast, but don't bunch up." I said.

Mac pulled back away from me, he was so close, that I could feel his warm breath passing by my ear. I took off my helmet to make the silhouette of my head much smaller and I slowly peaked around the corner, first looking down the right side, toward the enemy. I glanced quickly. Not only did I not know what was directly to my front, I ran the double risk of taking a shot to the back of the head from our own men on the other side. I pressed my sweaty brow against the cool clay of the corridor's wall. Pushing just my cheek out slightly, as if I were trying to extend just one eyeball out and around the corner, I jerked back suddenly when I heard the stomping footsteps of somebody running in my direction. Motioning for my team to stay put, I put my helmet back on, leaving the chinstrap dangling. My M-4 at the ready position, I could hear the footsteps getting progressively louder and closer together. Holding my rifle in my left hand using the advantage of the wall's natural cover to the best of my ability, I threw my left side out into the battle and just as I was about to take what would have been without question the most opportune shot I had ever before been offered by an enemy combatant, he halted before me. Wearing all black, with his face and head covered save for his eyes. He dove to the ground, falling to the prone position, he turned to his side, released the magazine from his weapon and began frantically inspecting his rifle. I didn't shoot at first, I still don't know why. I waited for him to put his magazine back in his rifle and for him to chamber a new round. As soon as he did, he collected his aim and I shot him.

"A guy came around the corner, I just shot him." I said.

"Let me get through, let me get up there, Sergeant." Mac said.

"No. Give me the radio." I said and he handed it to me.

I took a deep breath. My adrenaline was pumping so hard through my arms I could barely key the hand mic. "Yo Delta 1, this is Alpha 1. I got eyes on over."

"Roger, you got eyes on. Where are you? Over."

"We're right at the edge of the road down an alleyway, the same side as your gunner, about one hundred fifty meters up the road—break—we're gonna cross, go up, and pop smoke. How copy, over?"

"Roger, same side as my gunner hundred-fifty meters up. You're gonna cross and pop smoke on the roof. We'll be watching for you. Over."

"Roger that. When that smoke goes up, we'll lay down cover fire with everything we've got. Then move that MK19 up to our position, and bring whatever dismounts you got. How copy?"

"Negative on that last part, Drew. I got no guys for you. Repeat, I got no guys for you—break—I can bring the MK19 up, but all my guys are aiding casualties, over."

"Fuck. How bad is it back there, over?"

"Don't worry about it back here, Drew. Just help us push up and secure this road, then fall back to my position, over?"

"Roger. We gotta move. Alpha 1 out."

"Roger. Delta 1 out."

"Everybody, check your magazines. We're gonna move. When I get ten feet out, Mac, you follow me. Horton, Donaldson, you with me? We're gonna book it across. We just gotta be fast."

My breath was almost gone and I could barely get the words out.

"Fuck yeah, man, let's do this," Horton said.

"Roger Sergeant," Mac said.

"Okay, get ready. Wait, take off your NODS, we won't need 'em."

Mac relayed my message back. "Take off your NODs guys. Use your torches."

It was my fault as much as Donaldson or anybody's. I said nothing. I didn't hear Mac say anything either, or Horton. One of us should have said something, and it should have been me. I was in the front, I saw her first. A quick glance. A young petite girl, between fourteen and seventeen, her mother was also young. I passed them up, like I had been fortunate enough to pass up all the other unarmed non-combatants that were on the other side of some door I was kicking in. I had been lucky. While it holds true that in combat hesitation is the mother of all fuck ups, I had learned through hundreds of raids, that the vast majority of the people on the other side of the door had much more in common with that young mother and daughter than they did with the vicious Al-Qaeda insurgents we were there to fight. I heard the shot behind me and knew immediately what had happened. My first thought was that I was glad that it was not Mac. I could see him to my eight o' clock with my peripherals and was relieved, knowing that he could not handle another mistake like that.

Donaldson cried out, *"Sergeant. Oh my God, Sergeant!"*

"Donaldson, forget it. *Move!*" I yelled back at him. He was on his knees at the girl's shoulder, trying to hold her head up. The dead girl's mother was screaming incoherencies and throwing wild fists against Donaldson's oblivious helmet. I could imagine what her words might have been, *"What have you done? You monsters. You people are monsters. Look what you've done!"* She was dead though and we needed to move out.

I yelled, *"Horton, control that. Now goddamn it!"*

Horton was already barreling toward the disastrous scene. He came across with a running fist, knocking the woman cold with a swift punch across the jaw and in the same motion, hooked Donaldson up under the arm and pulled him up. *"We gotta move now, Don. Let's go."* He yelled. Not knowing if Donaldson was still in the fight or not, I turned around and ran for the stairs, worried that whoever was still in the building knew we were there.

The stairs were wooden and as I heard the stomping of four separate sets of feet, I knew that we were at full-strength and I ran up the stairs like it was day one of basic training. The stairs to the third floor were a separate set across the room from where we came. I feared the worst; it was a common living area. Beds and rugs on the floors everywhere, it looked to house three or four families, but nobody, thank Allah, was still there. Before running up to the rooftop I said, "Horton, you and Don block that stairwell door. Mac, follow me."

Mac and I made our way to the rooftop and a sudden sense of relief and salvation overtook me as I looked up at the starry night sky. The air was much fresher than it had been down below, it smelled sweet, without the stench of killing and dying. I took my last smoke grenade from its canister and released it toward the middle edge of the rooftop. Our building was higher than the surrounding ones, so the combatants on the other rooftops did not at first notice our position. I looked down across both sides to see dozens of enemy combatants firing small arms down at our troops on the street. The MK19 was couldn't do anything from where it was at but they couldn't move because they were protecting our downed casualties. We needed to advance somehow. We could only imagine the horrific scene down below.

Our best chance was to use the advantage of our elevated position and rain down with a as much fire as four men could lay down. *"Mac, go get those two. Hurry. We need to hit these fuckers hard and all at once,"* I yelled.

The assault was quick and precise and except for a few stragglers, the four of us cleared the ambush sight. Thinking back now, I won't say that we fought bravely, because after going through two wars, I have little to say regarding the virtue of bravery. I will say that we were fierce and we were swift, and that is why we are alive and our enemies are not.

CHAPTER FOUR
Tourniquets

THE PART OF THE fight that would earn us our medals was over. The part that I think about the most was still to come. I don't think that night ever really ended. At least for Donaldson, the worst was over. He was a reserved paratrooper to put it mildly. To put it plainly, a person with his almost inability to turn off his moral faculties had no business being in the infantry. Maybe I didn't either.

As we came upon the wreckage, my chest sank and my skin became cool and numb to touch. Neither me, nor any of my men had ever before been on the bad end of such an effective ambush. I knew what so many of my enemies must have felt like over the last three years. I had experienced something that does not fall on the shoulders of all or even most infantrymen of the modern era.

We had been completely surrounded by the enemy. In every direction, between us and our fellow soldiers, there were enemy forces heavily fortified and aching to kill our entire team. There was no hope for aid or reinforcements. We had no air support, no indirect fire support. The rest of our platoon was completely cut off at best. It was just the four of us, and whatever they had out there. But narrowly escaping this debacle was what I remember least vividly about the night.

The second Humvee was destroyed so severely that I could barely tell the front from the back. The tires had been blown almost completely off their wheels, and both axles were broken so the body of the truck sank down and was laying almost flat with the ground.

All that was left of the inside was of the burnt wire framings of the seats. You could hear the crackle of still lit materials, and it smelled like burnt plastic.

Sergeant Cantrell, was leading the rear and only still operational truck; the third truck was also disabled from the initial blast, as were the soldiers, all killed or seriously wounded. It was then that I learned that some of the men from the middle two trucks were still alive. All of Cantrell's men, except for a MK19 gunner placing precise rounds for our cover, were busy aiding our wounded soldiers. It was only then that I knew we'd make it out alive. There was more to be done though, and the worst in many ways, was yet to come.

We were tired but the rest of the platoon needed our help. My men reacted quickly.

"Mac, go help out," I said.

"Roger, on it, Sergeant."

I could barely hear the last word. Mac was already running with his aid bag in-hand.

Sergeant Cantrell approached me with a look of total stoicism. His first name was Arthur and he was a tall blonde southerner who carried no accent, but was proud to be from 'Dixie Land' as he called it. He had come to the unit two years ago, transferring from a tank unit. He was amongst the soldiers who initially invaded in 2003.

It was unusual for both of us, but we liked each other from the beginning. I hadn't known him the longest, but he was perhaps my closest friend. The mere sight of his face was a necessary comfort in an otherwise hellish night. He wore less expression than I had ever seen before. His lips were thin, his jaw distinct. He had the smile of a plastic toy action figure. But not on that night. I didn't know what was going on in the wreckage while we were cut off, but one look from his dimmed eyes hinted at the horror.

"Art...fuck man. What the fuck happened?" I asked.

"They fucking got us. They hit us hard." He panned up from my boots to my armor, wondering I'm sure, but not asking of the origin of the massive blood stains painting my pant leg.

"Who's alive?" I asked.

"Mason. Stevens, maybe."

"Where the fuck's the LT? I didn't see him anywhere."

Cantrell just stared down the road toward the sporadic muzzle flashes from the couple of die-hards still in the fight. That's what we called the ones that didn't give up or run, the "die-hards". That kind of resolve was usually welcomed. But that night was different, we were hurt badly, many dead, and we were all tired and wanted an assessment of our downed brothers. Everything was different that night.

Right then I realized that it was the first time that somebody really got the drop on me. I'd been sniped at before, a couple IED's, even an ambush, but there was a precision to this strike and it worked. We were all defeated in a way. At least that was how I felt. I was still alive, we all were. I looked at my men as they moved and felt like a father who had not been there for his children. I was not the leader that I wish they could have had. But I don't know what I would have done differently.

"You give my guy a break on the MK19?" Cantrell asked.

"Yeah, of course." I pulled out my hand mic, "Alpha 2 this is Alpha 1…" I said and keyed my hand mic looking at Cantrell the whole time. "Horton, come in."

"Go 'head 1."

"Send Don on to relieve Alpha 3's guy off that MK19."

"Roger, Sergeant."

"Just have him go take a knee; tell him to have a smoke. 1 out."

"Roger, out."

I knew that he didn't want to answer my question, so I waited a second before I asked it again. "Where's the LT?"

He stared down the dark road in the direction of his MK19 gunner. We watched as his guy got down and Horton went up. Cantrell's Private, I don't remember his name, ran toward us and Cantrell put his hand up slowly and motioned for him to stop running and the Private quickly slowed to a walk and he breathed out so deeply that I could hear him from where I was. This kid was not a day over 19. I don't think he really had to shave yet. I couldn't imagine what he'd seen while we were doing what we were. It must have been bad. Cantrell looked at him like he'd never seen him before in his life. "Sergeant?" The young Private asked.

Cantrell stood and said nothing and just stared at Horton who was now manning the MK19. "Go get some water." I said to the Private.

"Sergeant?" he asked.

"Move out, Private!" He took his hand off the pistol grip of his rifle and let it hand in front of him from its sling and reached his hand down and pulled a canteen and drank from it. I looked over at Cantrell who was still just staring at Horton. I should have gone over to him but I just yelled his name.

"Dude…Cant….*Cant!*" I yelled.

He kept staring at the truck. "He's in there."

Without looking in the direction, he pointed across his body to the other side of the road. There was a dimly lit room in a small building where a soldier was standing guard on one knee. The doorway was black, but I could see a faint light coming from the inside. I looked at Cantrell, but said nothing, he would not have responded if I had.

An older than average private named Edwards stood guard on bended knee at the door. He was new to the platoon as most of the privates were and I knew him only by name. His face was pale white, glowing in the night's dark. His eyes were spread wide as if taped open involuntarily. I said nothing to him as I approached the door. He raised his head as I walked by, but never enough to look into my eyes.

I could hear the muffled screams of the Lieutenant well before I walked into the light. The anticipation was terrible but short. Almost immediately my imaginings were replaced by the grimness of reality. His words were the precursor to what I was about to see in full light. The LT was being held down by each shoulder by two privates who weren't old enough to legally drink. A third private, one of our platoon's attached medics from headquarters company, was doing everything he could to stop the bleeding. I cannot begin to imagine the level of terror he was experiencing. He yelled it over and over again, *"My legs. Get my legs. Don't leave my legs."*

Doc Menendez struggled to apply the tourniquets. When somebody loses a limb to an IED, they don't usually lose the limb right away, not all of it anyway. There is no clean cut where the leg was neatly separated and detached. His legs were still connected to his body. Ligaments and tendons usually hold things together enough to provide an even more horrific sight than if the legs were just completely gone. You could barely tell the difference between the shattered blood soaked bone and torn apart tendon that looked like thick cables with bits of tattered flesh hanging off of them. It was obvious that even if Doc could stop the bleeding that he'd lose both legs. He reassured him that he'd be fine and the LT knew that he wouldn't but he became calm somehow anyway and he reached up with a powerful grip and said to Doc, "Just fix me up really quick Doc, so you can get out there and help the other men."

Doc reached his hand up to his shoulder to reach the LT's and put it on top of it and said, "Your men are doing just fine, Sir. A couple of nicks and bruises is all. Ain't that right, Sergeant. Hey, Sergeant."

I didn't even realize he was talking to me. I couldn't believe what I was seeing, the bravery of both these men was something I try to hold with me and remind me how honorable some of us were.

"The men are fine, Sir, just taking care of the last few fuckers running around out there. We're gonna get every fucking one of 'em, Sir." All I could think about is how I should have been in his spot. Doc snapped me back.

"Sergeant, I need you to give me a hand here. If you can handle it," Doc said.

"What do you need from me, Doc?"

I didn't know what he was going to have me do. I didn't know what I was going to be able to do.

"I need you to help me readjust these tourniquets right now. He's losing too much blood," he said.

The room we were in was empty except for one old torn-up chair in the corner. The LT was lying on the ground on top of a small tarp.

"I need you to hold these up real quick." He said.

His pants were soaked in blood and peppered with shrapnel holes all the way up to the waist band. I held them up and away from his body by pulling on the belt loops. Doc cut along the seams with medical scissors, exposing his groin and multiple additional shrapnel wounds.

"I have to get these off him and get these tourniquets tighter. The LT's body thrashed around on the ground and dust swirled around the whole room.

Doc yelled out, *"You need to hold him down goddamnit!"*

I don't know how, but the LT was fighting with everything he had to sit up.

"Hold him the fuck down!" I yelled at the privates.

"I'm trying, Sergeant." A private answered.

"So fucking do it now goddamn it!" I screamed and was as angry at the private as I was at whoever hit us.

"I'm sorry, sir." Doc said to the LT.

He pushed his shoulder down with all his force and put a knee down onto it and grabbed his forehead and held him to the ground.

"You're legs are gonna be fine, sir. Just need some R&R. Now, I gotta tighten these up now sir, it's going to hurt for a minute. I need you to get ready," Doc said and he looked up at me and shifted his weight to his other knee.

"Okay Sergeant, I just need you to help hold him now. He's gonna wanna move a lot."

"Okay, I got it man, just tell me when." I looked down at the LT and he nodded and said, "Do it, just do it now, I'm ready."
Alright hold him down, now," said Doc and as soon as he cranked down on the first tourniquet, the LT's body went as stiff as a hickory board and then right away limp.

"Holy fuck, Doc," I yelled out. *"I think he's dead!"*

"He's just passed out. It's fine," said Doc calmly.

"Jesus Fucking Christ, Doc. What the fuck?" I said.

"Thanks, Sergeant. I got it from here. You don't have to stay, Sergeant," he said.

I was still down on my knees holding onto the LT. I looked up at Doc with nothing to say. My mouth was wide open, but nothing came out. The same disoriented nausea I experienced before came rushing back to me. I stood up and walked outside and threw up. I wiped my mouth with the back of my sleeve and spit twice. I went back inside where the Doc and LT were and asked, "You want me to send in Mac? He's our best man at first aid."

"No. I got it, Sergeant. I don't want anybody else to see him like this," he said.

"The Medevac will be here real soon. Good work, Doc. Is he gonna make it?" I asked.

Still down on his knees he had covered the LT up with a poncho liner and was pouring a bottle of water over his blood-stained hands.

"I don't know. Maybe," he said.

"You did everything you could here tonight, Doc. Whatever happens."

"Roger, Sergeant."

That was my last combat operation. That was Mac's last combat operation. They had won. I was still alive, so was Mac, and the rest of my men too. But that was it for me. I never went out again. It would have been just the same for them if they would have killed me. Either way, my fight was over. For my actions, I was given my fourth

Army Commendation Medal. Mac got his third. He deserved much more. The LT was given a bronze star and two prosthetic legs.

CHAPTER FIVE
When the Fighting Stops

AFTER FIVE MONTHS OF the thickest fighting since the Tet Offensive, our battalion returned to Fort Bragg twenty-six men light. That means that about one in nine of us were killed, a quarter more were wounded or injured. It was so much more than that though. We all carried something back. Maybe it was the degree or the consistency of the fighting, but we all lost something. Some of us knew right away, and some of us it took longer for the seams to break. I thought when I came home that I'd be able to pick up all the broken pieces. It was harder than I could have ever imagined.

We flew into Fort Bragg on a warm Friday morning. From Bahram Airfield in Iraq, we went to Ramstein Airfield where we have bases in Germany. We spent a day there but didn't leave the base. The flight from Germany to Fort Bragg lasted about thirteen hours. Most of us slept the whole way. But a few stragglers still looked around the plane at the empty seats and remembered that on the way there, it was so full that the lowest privates had to sit and lay on the ground.

Two hours after turning in our gear and being released to the outside world for a four day weekend, our platoon sergeant, Sergeant First Class Hawk, called me to his office and thanked me for what I had done during this last tour and then told me I was relieved of my leadership over Alpha team.

That was it, no more team leading, no more responsibility. I was short-timing and they didn't want any of my half assed attitude rubbing off on the rest of the guys. It was the right thing to do but it bothered me all the same. The timing seemed to be in poor taste but the army isn't worried about any one soldier's sensibilities, it can't be. That was kind of my general attitude toward the army at that point, I had seen enough to know it was the way it was because it needed to be that way, but I didn't want to be a part of it anymore. Maybe I wasn't quite the man I went out to prove that I was. I didn't care anymore.

Paved roads and traffic lights were a new thing. It took about three miles before I remembered I had a radio that played music. I remember sweating. An unfamiliar but severe pain in the pit of my stomach began to throb and expand through my whole body. By the time I got home, I was soaked in sweat and felt like vomiting was inevitable. I hadn't eaten since Germany so I just dry heaved into the concrete of my apartment parking lot for a couple of minutes. Curious onlookers watched my combat uniformed body pushing out all the bad things they didn't have to ever know about. I sat on the edge of the curb next to my car and pulled out my phone but didn't have anybody in mind to call. My stomach was as empty as it had ever been and I was weak and my knees nearly buckled as I tried to stand. I sat back down on the curb and collected myself for a couple of minutes before I tried again and was able to walk in a semi straight line toward the place I once shared with my ex-wife.

The apartment was empty except for the couch and television set my ex-wife had been so kind as to leave me. There was also a small coffee table in front of the couch, but no remote control on top so I turned on the TV by pressing the button on the set but there was no signal and all I got was white noise. The fridge was empty. The bed sat with no sheets or blankets, my clothes hung in the closet and a pile of extra field gear was shoved into the far corner. I took off the uniform that I'd been wearing every day for the last half year and walked around naked until I realized I didn't have any towels. I put my dessert pants back on, buttoning them but not fastening my belt. I put my bare feet back into my boots but didn't tie them and I walked out my door and back down to my car. I opened up the duffel bag I'd been living out of and looked for an Army issued olive drab green towel so I could clean my sweaty body.

I showered for thirty minutes. You forget about little luxuries like hot water. It felt good, but I was ruffled when I saw my ex-wife's sky blue loofa still hanging from the faucet. The first night back from my other tours had been spent between her legs. I wiped the steam from the mirror and took notice of my shrunken reflection. I'd missed too many meals and lost too many nights over the last few months and I didn't look like the hulking warrior I remembered from before I left. She probably wouldn't even think I looked good anymore anyway. That's what I thought about anyway, what I'd lost over there, and it was a lot more than some muscle mass and my ipod. A wife, another bit of my soul, a life? I didn't know how much yet.

Several phone calls came in from the guys in the platoon. I answered none of them. The boys in the barracks would be drinking till seven a.m., sleep till three and then start again. The single sergeants would do the same in the bars and the married guys would either fuck their wives or say 'fuck' their wives. I didn't get a chance to do either.

I drove to a part of town that soldiers didn't really go and noticed her immediately, but waited several drinks before approaching. Luck was on my side as she had made herself inimitably approachable with a combination of seductive expressions that involved her gently biting her bottom lip with her top teeth in a manner usually reserved for actresses of the adult film industry. We exchanged deliberate looks from across the crowded and conversation busy bar. Along with the mouth stuff, she would drop one shoulder and extend her neck out while turning her head slightly to the side as if I were a vampire she was inviting to have a taste. I hadn't drank in months, so I already felt the effect from the three beers I had, but only to the degree that it gave me confidence to exercise a part of myself that I hoped my ex-wife hadn't taken with her. More than anything, it was a way to not think about what had or was happening. Sex is great for distraction, better than any drug. Not always as easy to find though, or as cheap.

"It must just be so scary over there. I can't even imagine."

"I don't know…you're just there to do a job. Don't think about much else I guess."

"Well you can't really. I mean you have to just like, block it all out I'm sure, right?" Her legs were crossed atop the high barstool. She crossed them slowly the other way like an actress in a Paul Verhoeven film. She noticed as my eyes fell to her tan thighs. She wore a black finger-tip length dress that clung to her figure in a manner that distracted from whatever she was saying.

Ashley wasn't the kind of girl you'd want to take home to your mom, but she was definitely the kind of girl you wanted to take home to your bed. Some girls have that 'fuck me six ways to Sunday look' naturally, and some try hard to achieve it with makeup and short dresses. Ashley had both and after a few drinks and five months without sex, she might as well have been Barbarella herself. The mere anticipation of feeling her naked body against mine was enough to numb my fingertips. It doesn't matter who it's with, when you're young, every new lover is a discovery of not just that person but even more so of yourself.

The surest way to get laid as a soldier was to talk about combat. There are two approaches to this: one, you can play the tough guy and act like a hardened commando that is immune to all feeling. This will get you laid by girls who go to community college and are most concerned about a man's abdominal muscles. The second approach requires much more wherewithal because you have to be slightly withdrawn, suggesting an underlying sentimentality while still staying emotionally engaged in the conversation. The girl has to think that you are badass enough to go fight on the front line, but at the same time, sensitive enough to have those experiences weigh on your conscience when you get back. This will get you laid by the girl who attends an actual university and watches foreign films. Knowing nothing of Ashley other than that she had a tattoo of three stars on the top of her left foot and her toes were painted with blue nail polish, I used the first approach.

"Yeah, I don't know. It's like everything just hits you later on, you know? Like when you're out on a patrol, or a mission, and shit goes down, you take fire or an IED goes off or whatever; you're fine, then you just react and do what you need to do, what you were trained to do. There's no time to think about what's next; you just have to do it, or you and a lot of other people are going to die." Her eyes were wide and she nodded with an exaggerated interest. It was working. And to be fair, there was truth in what I said, but the words still made me a little sick as I said them. I pushed her brightly colored fruit cocktail a bit closer to her freshly manicured hands and took a big drink from my beer bottle, more as a way to give me just a moment to think of the next thing to say. Ashley was not much for discourse. She abstained from any word over two syllables and whenever the conversation stopped for more than five seconds, she looked curiously around the room as if she were contemplating her whereabouts. Her breasts were small but her dress held them high and close together which provided them with a look of breasts twice the size, and they were shaped nice, which is much more important than the size of the breast. As I think of her breasts and what they must look like under that push up bra, I realize that her name has escaped me. Don't panic, I tell myself, it won't matter anyway. Just keep talking until it's time to kiss her.

She was dumb, even for a party girl. She had some glitter on her face that I noticed when I got a bit closer, which turned me on at first, but only at first. Girls who wear glitter on their faces are easy to fuck. Her hair was as dark as her dress. It fell in loose curls down past her attentive breasts. Her eyes were the bright blue of the morning sky. She had sex appeal more than anything else. I won't say that Ashley was beautiful, she was just too petite. A small woman cannot be beautiful, she can be pretty and definitely provocative, but she cannot be beautiful. Ashley was hot though, there is no other way to say it.

I wanted more than anything to close the small gap that separated our faces. We were crowded at the bar and I began to sweat from both the heat and the angst of being pressed against others as impatient bar patrons reached over me and between us, practically begging for drinks. I finished my fourth drink and ordered her another cocktail and I was becoming increasingly anxious about the large crowd accumulating around us, but there was nowhere else to sit but at the bar and I thought it best to hold what ground I had.

She had earlier carried the scent of summer melon, but now I was close enough to smell the rum coming off her lips and tongue. As she spoke I watched her face more than listened to her words. I finally had her talking only to realize I did not at all care what she said. Her presence drew me like a magnet, a slow steady pull. The last woman I had been this close to was the one Donaldson shot in the head a few days before. Ashley's lips were inviting and my gaze dropped to her mouth. They were pink and glowed under the dim bar room lighting. She parted them only slightly. Her jaw was sharp and as she spoke she loosened her face into a smile that got wider as her sentences ran on. I moved my bar stool closer and widened my shoulders in an attempt to detract people from coming next to me.

Her smell made me think of the wife I had lost. There is nothing quite so crystalline as the memories evoked by the olfactory senses. Something about the combination of department store fruit scented lotion and hard liquor struck an angered familiarity that I did not at the moment recognize as such. I tried not thinking of my wife, in combat it was easier to do because was halfway around the world, but now, I knew she was close, probably in the same town still. All that was over now though and I knew it and had no real ambition of fixing things. Our relationship had run its course and I'm glad that she was the one who ended it. For whatever reason though, at that moment, I wished it was her I was with and not Ashley. Maybe I just wanted something familiar. Maybe I did miss her. My body missed her; I missed her presence, but not particularly *her* presence. Just familiar presence, it just happened to be hers that I knew. Ashley had turned from a girl I hoped to fuck to a girl that I was pissed at for not being my wife. She was carrying on about something regarding school when I made my turn. Something about nursing I remember.

"So Ashley, let me ask you, why do you want to be a nurse? I mean I get that you like helping people or whatever, you said all that and that's really nice and all but there're other ways to help people. You could be a teacher, or a social worker, or a guidance counselor, tons of stuff."

She cut me off with a quick smile. "Or a soldier, right?"

I didn't know if she was serious or being fatuous. I smiled back just a little and kept on.

"But really, I mean, why nursing exactly?" I insisted on a more satisfactory answer.

She brought her lips tightly together and sucked both of them in so that they practically disappeared. Her eyes widened and focused on nothing in particular. I sat back on my stool with crossed arms and an impatient anticipation.

"I don't know, I guess I just like taking care of people. You know?" She smiled and tonged the end of her straw before bringing it to her lips. Her answer was completely unacceptable and I dug back in like a determined trial attorney.

"Well, yeah, but that's kind of the same thing as saying you like helping people, that you like taking care of people. I mean really, it's the same thing." My arms became tighter across my chest and I leaned in with staunch determination. The passion I had earlier was replaced by unbridled rage. She finally sensed the change in demeanor. Ashley wasn't too bright.

"Well, why did you join the army, wasn't it to help people?" She asked with her lip curled and with a slight whimpering of hesitancy.

I felt her weakness and fired hard, "No, not at all really. I didn't care about helping people. I wanted to kill people. That's why I joined the infantry." I answered and her mouth dropped at the sides.

Whatever Ashley's mental faculties might have been, her heart was good and pure and I recognized that even then, and at the time it fed my cutting scorn. She wasn't as easily shaken as she might have been. She anchored herself in her seat and she seemed to grow three inches taller as her back straightened and her back arched and her head rose to the level of mine. She spoke with a new determined confidence and asked, "But you wanted to kill bad people, right? Terrorists and stuff, right?" She set her drink on the bar in front of her hand and made a loose fist and put her other hand on top of it. She watched as I looked at her, confused at first and not knowing how to react.

"I don't know. Not really. I don't think I really thought about that stuff very much. I went for me, so I could go to war and see what it was like. We could have been going to war against Canada, I'd have gone no matter what," I said. I had never thought about that until she had just asked me in that very moment.

"Yeah but I mean, you're like a strong guy and stuff, being a soldier for you is like me being a nurse," she said. There was an edge to her words that were softer before. I decided to meet her tone with hostility of course.

"What the fuck are you even talking about? Look, you being a nurse and me being a soldier isn't even the same fucking thing. I wanted to kill people, you wanted to help people. I didn't give a fuck about 9-11 to tell you the truth. All that shit was to me was a sure ticket to combat, being a fucking man, that's what I thought anyway." I laughed after I said it and took a drink of my beer. Ashley sat back in her seat and crossed her arms and looked at me as though she hadn't understood a word I said. She was patient, she would probably make a great nurse.

A space had separated us. Both leaned back in our stools as far as we could be, arms tightly crossed, eyes locked, she smiled and her shoulders dropped and she leaned forward and while putting her hands on top of my forearms like she wanted to pry them apart she said, "You protect people though, I'm keeping people healthy. We're more alike than you think." I could have kissed her right then. That's what I should have done. Somehow, that's still what she wanted me to do.

"We are nothing alike, Ashley." I said in contempt.

She sat back in her chair and dropped her head to the side. I turned to look at her for the and said, "First off, most nurses I see aren't keeping anybody healthy, more just keeping people alive when they should be dead already. Second..." I had nothing else. I took a drink of my beer and looked away from her. I heard the half melted ice cubes against the empty glass as she set her drink down and I turned to her and said, "I'll get you another one?"

I was already signaling the bartender even though she had said no. I didn't even want her to stay, but I was busy, occupied with something other than my thoughts, so I was insistent and she complied. The bartender must have seen that she didn't want another drink because he ignored me. He went on rubbing a highball glass with a towel like he was tending bar in some old west saloon.

He looked at me but said nothing until finally I called out to him, "Let me get two more over here." I called out.

He was a young man but still older than myself. He did not ignore me but didn't respond verbally. He nodded slightly in my direction then looked away immediately and continued to trace the rim of the glass with his little white towel. I frothed at the mouth like a rabid hound and jumped out of my bar stool quickly enough to turn a few people in my direction. I had the bartender's attention but he still did not approach me.

Ashley clenched my arm firmly without squeezing it and said in a kind of reserved panic, "It's okay. I don't really want another drink anyway. It's getting pretty late and I have work tomorrow morning anyway."

I looked at her with a disgust she hadn't earned and slowly panned over to the bartender. I traced him as he went around the bar collecting empty glasses. He was smiling slightly now and moving his head to the music that I was too angry to register. Ashley squeezed my arm as tightly as her hand probably could.

I snapped my head around to her and said, "It's fine. One more, he'll get it for us."

Her grip loosened and she took on a maternal charm that would have made many men fall in love with her right then and there. She was probably a very good nurse.

"Really, it's fine. I really don't even want another one," she said.

"We're getting one more, just hold on." I said.

"No. I'm going to go home now. It was really nice talking to you, Drew." I could tell that she was a little scared and I felt bad about making that happen.

"So, what? Now you're leaving?" I asked as if confused. She looked nervous and put her hand out for me to shake. I did not.

"Well, okay. I'll see you later, I guess. Nice to meet you," she said.

I said nothing back.

"Okay. Bye, Drew," she said in a sorrowful voice and walked away quickly and the bartender set a single beer down next to me.

I looked up at his straight lips and beading eyes and he said to me in a deliberate voice, "Five dollars." We exchanged stares. At that point what bothered me more than anything was that he didn't submit. Didn't he know where I'd been and what I'd had done, just two weeks before? He didn't care. It was not his world.

I put down a five-dollar bill and left.

CHAPTER SIX
Fayettenam

ANXIOUS HEARTBEATS AND PANICKED breaths took over my whole body. Both my underarms were damp with stale sweat and the tasted of stale cigarettes lined my mouth. Little collections of perspiration gathered all around my hands where my fingers gripped the steering wheel. My eyes looked like somebody had thrown granulated soap in them minutes ago. My hands were not all there for me and I had trouble lighting my cigarette. I dropped my lighter in my lap and was fumbling for it in a stupor as I felt my car pulling to the side by a slight bend in the road's curve. I was startled when I could feel my tires slipping on the loose gravel. A rush of blood shot to my crotch of all places and I distinctly remember a sensation on my scalp that felt like nothing else than a giant millipede treading across my skull. My car began to fishtail and brought me conveniently back on the road as it started to straighten. I felt a cold rush make its way from the back of my neck down to my tailbone and then back up again. I looked once again into the mirror to see a whirlwind of dust bellowing out from around the car and I laughed and lit my cigarette and drove on even faster. Both windows were rolled down and the wind hit my face with a cooling force as my adrenaline levels began to fall.

It was a quarter or so past two when I got home. Ashley had left me four hours and three bars ago. The rest of my night went without incident. I have a faint recollection of a disagreement with another soldier, but that cannot be for certain. All the blood in my body felt as though it had collected in the front of my face. My breath could start a fire. When I finally stopped, I was at least sober enough to notice that I hadn't had my headlights on the whole time. I had violently shouted out of my window at a couple of passing cars that had flashed their lights on me. My hands and feet were numb with drunken exhaustion. I wanted more to drink and remembered that my fridge was empty. The bars were all closed, which was why I came home. I went to the gas station up the road that also sold beer and wine. Part of me hoped to run into somebody like me so maybe I could try to beat the hell out of them. There probably was some disagreement earlier but I cannot be certain.

My apartment was just off a main road in Fayetteville, NC. If there were any good parts in Fayetteville, I certainly did not live in one of them. My place was about ten miles outside of post and as it is with practically every military town, Fayetteville displayed all the poverty, violence, and cheap indulgence of a major metropolitan without providing the accompanying art, culture, or sophistication.

Between my apartment complex and the gas station just up the way were two other apartment complexes. The one I lived in was almost exclusively soldiers and their spouses. The next place was an even mixture of soldiers, community college students, and young blue collars. I was walking by the third complex when I was drawn into a group of five black men standing by the bus stop next to the entrance. No soldiers lived there. The apartments were on a list of restricted housing areas in division, which meant that no commander would sign off on a soldier's request to live off post if it was going to be at a residence in that apartment complex.

I walked up to them and said, "Hey ya there guys. Nice night...eh, isn't it now?" I never would have stopped to talk to these guys. Never had even said hello in passing. For whatever reason, for the first time, I didn't see them as different than me.

None of them said anything right away, they looked more confused than anything else. They looked at each other and then a couple of them looked down at themselves, almost as if to see if they had spilled something on their shirts. Then one of them looked up at the sky and then back down at me and said, "Yeah homie, starry and shit."

He was holding the joint and looked back up and all our heads followed his like we were in church or something.

"Yeah man, all clear and shit like this, looks like a, uh, night in fuckin' Iraq, you know," I said.

"You a soldier; you just back from there, man?" another asked. Before I could answer, his friend chimed in fast, "What the fuck you think, stupid? Can't you tell the man's a goddamn soldier? Look at that haircut and shit, man," another answered.

"Got back this—sorry there, excuse me, just this week, man." My speech jerked with the 'hicks' and burps of a cartoon drunk.

"No shit. Welcome back homie," the first one said.

"Yeah, welcome back, man," the second one said.

"For real, welcome home," the third one said.

"Welcome back, man," said another.

"Yo, thanks for what you do, man," said another.

I was waiting for something more to happen. For the mood to change, their posturing, something—but it never did. They were as genuine of people that I could remember ever speaking to.

"Na na na na, na na na, it's just a job. It's all it is. It's just a job," I said as I let my head carelessly explore my shoulders.

"Yeah, fuck all that man. I work at fucking Subway, man. I ain't about to strap on for those motherfuckers, that's for goddamn sure." I didn't want to talk about it anymore and just laughed with everybody else. They kept passing what I could now see was a blunt and not a joint.

"Where you live at homie?" the second one asked.

"Oh, just down the fuck'n road, man. Not this one," I pointed, "Next one down," I said.

"Oh shit, you staying in lil' Bragg?" the first one said.

"The fuck's Little Bragg?" I asked.

"Where all you soldiers live, homie," the first one said.

"Yeah, I guess it is just soldiers, and their fucking wives too. And—kids," I said.

"So why ya'll live down there? How come none you ever live up over here?" another asked.

"*I* wanted to. *They* wouldn't let me. The fuckers!" I said and spit to the side.

They all laughed and waited for me to say something else. For whatever reason, I seemed to be entertaining and it felt good to want to talk to somebody without stripes on their collar. I went on with my drunken ramblings as they silently nodded and laughed amongst themselves.

"I looked at a place here. I was going to move in and shit too. Rent's way fuckin' cheaper, and they're just as nice too. They really fuckin' are," I said.

"I don't know about all that," the third one said and laughed to himself. He was the most talkative and was smiling from the moment I walked up. At least as drunk as me, he danced a little as he moved, kind of chubby but wore it well so you wouldn't call him fat.

"Well, I mean they're pretty much as nice. I mean you guys don't have a pool and as much grass and shit around, but the inside of the apartments are pretty much just the same. And I don't give a fuck about swimmin' or looking at fuckin' grass." I said.

"Yeah, no shit," another one said.

I turned toward him and continued, "Yeah, so I was going to move in, got a lease and everything. Don't know if you guys know, but we gotta get fucking approval—sorry, man, these goddamn hiccups," I pounded my chest as if to knock them out of my body and went on, "To live off base," I said.

"Get the fuck outta here. What?" the second one asked.

"No shit, dude. Gotta get approval. Not just permission; you gotta bring your fuckin' company commander a copy of your lease and shit, and then they check it all out and let you know if it's okay for you to sign it," I said.

"You have to do this when you move *off* post?" the first one asked.

"Fuckin'-A right," I said.

"That don't make no goddamn sense," he said.

"It's how it is though man. This man's fuckin' army, I'm telling you. I got a copy of my lease and brought it back for the C.O. to check out and the shit got rejected right away. I thought something might be up and they weren't going to let me move off base anymore, but what happened was, this apartment complex here is on a list of a dozen or so places we can't live," I said.

"Ya'll motherfuckers, aren't *allowed* to live here?" another asked. Everyone else was quiet. The blunt still moved along.

"Nope," I said and lit another cigarette and smoked it talking to only one of the men as the rest politely ignored me and talked amongst themselves. I finished my cigarette and exchanged goodbyes with each one before continuing to the store.

They had put me in a good mood for a short time but there was a bit of bad noise at the gas station that turned me nasty again. The clerk wasn't willing to sell me booze on account of the time. After a bit of a stir I brought up that I had just gotten back from my third tour; he sold to me with the sole condition that I wouldn't ever come back to his store.

The walk back felt much longer; it always does. The guys I'd talked to were gone by then and all but a couple of lights were off along the whole street. It was as still a moment as I had had in five months. No gunfire. No radio traffic, not even vehicle traffic, no fucking helicopters, or running generators. Just the still of the night. I think I may have even heard crickets. Combat doesn't afford many moments alone and as my thoughts drifted back, it all tightened up on me again. I took a beer from the six-pack and drank half of it down right away.

Maybe I should have gone out with some of the guys. Things were different for me because I wasn't a career guy and they all were. Everybody talks about getting out; we all did. Nobody really believes anybody until it happens though and that time had come for me and I was somebody else to them. None of us got exactly what they wanted from going to war; that I know for sure. Apparently, I had gotten much less though. The killing was part of the job, we all knew that coming in and most of us wanted to do that specifically; it's why we signed up for the infantry. You have to remember, we were mostly all kids of the eighties, the Reagan years, the Schwarzenegger years. Violence was all around us, celebrated in Hollywood and propagandized by the media. And we were boys, American boys raised to be American men, men who are strong and tough and stoic and fight. But it wasn't so much in the fighting, it was all the other stuff that they never really show in the movies, like children getting run over by speeding Humvees and civilians getting caught up in crossfire and blown apart by mortar rounds that fell too long or too short, and that's just the accidental stuff.

Somehow, twice as drunk by the time I got back, I sat in the dark on the floor against the refrigerator. The cold stainless-steel door felt good against my back, so I took off my shirt to feel it proper. I smoked three more cigarettes and called my mother who I'd spoken to only briefly while waiting in line for the arms room to turn in my weapon hours ago. I wanted to talk to my mom. Never in my life have I met someone who possessed all the wonderful, and regretfully unrewarded virtues of humankind. She was the kind of person who would apologize to out of town guests for the poor weather—and meant it. She'd never wanted me to join the army, but never said a bad word about it.

"Hello." My mother's voice was rough like gravel when she woke, but still soothing in its reminiscence. Three tours had done as much to her as it had to me.

"Hi mom. Sorry it's so late."

"It's okay, Drew. Is everything alright? I thought you'd be asleep by now."

"Yeah. Everything's fine. Everything's good. What are you doing?"

"Well, just sleeping. It's really late there, Drew. What are you still doing up? You must be exhausted?"

"Oh, I was just watching movies. I couldn't really go to sleep. I can call tomorrow."

"No. It's fine. You can call me anytime, day or night. You know that. I just didn't expect to hear from you again until tomorrow, I'm glad that you called though, Drew. Did they tell you when you can come home on leave yet?"

"No, but I don't think I'm going to take leave anyway, I'm just going to sign out a week or so early, since I'm getting out anyway."

"I just can't wait to see you, Drew. And to have you home now, and safe.

She began to cry and I did too and I wished she was there. I didn't want her to know I was crying too, so I started talking again right away.

"Maybe I'll take a trip somewhere when I get out." I said.

"Where would you go?" She asked with great curiosity.

"I was thinking about how Grandma was always talking about Milan; about how much she missed it and hoped that we could all go back together some day." I loved my grandmother's stories about Italy.

"Yeah, I wish we could have gone back there with her. Life has a way of getting really complicated though." Her excited curiosity had turned to a drab mumbling.

My mother missed her more than anybody. I think she was the only person who ever listened to her.

"You remember what she always said about it? About how the people were always happy and talking on the streets and they were always so clean and how it only rained when it made the city more beautiful. Remember how she used to always say that?" I asked.

"I do." She softly confirmed.

"And then she would go on about how you couldn't get a good calzone in America and how the only thing worse than French wine was California wine." I said.

My mother laughed a kind of sad laugh.

"Your grandmother loved you so much, Drew." She said.

"I know. I really miss her sometimes." I always missed my grandmother when I thought of her.

"She'll always be with you." I didn't like it when people said stuff like that. Especially when I knew they didn't really believe it. We both fell silent for a long few seconds. I could hear my father saying something in the background.

"What did Dad say? What's he saying?" I asked.

"Nothing. He's just getting out of bed," my mom said.

"I can hear him talking."

I often heard my father in the background as if he were my mother's doppelganger, barking the ungraceful words of a harsher parent.

"Hold on, your father wants to talk to you."

"About what?"

"Oh, Drew. He just wants to say hi," she said in a muffled voice that I'm sure my father still heard.

"Fine,"I said. My father coughed into the phone and started in like he'd been awake for hours.

"What are you doing up still, Drew?"

"How are you doing, Dad?"

"Well it's late, Drew."

"Yeah I know. You can go back to bed if you want, I can talk to mom."

"You can talk to her in a minute. She went into the bathroom to get some headache medicine."

My mom often got headaches, she really did. And it wasn't that I didn't want to talk to my dad, it's that I didn't know what to say to him. Neither of us had known how to act toward each other for a long time. But he was the one who taught me to be tough. Not just strong, but lasting. The tragedy was that in the amidst of a world where superficiality is favored over authenticity; even his only son would never express his admiration.

"Remember the picture in the living room, Dad, of the moon landing?" I asked.

"Yeah, it's still there," he said.

I laughed a little bit, but I don't know why.

"What about it, Drew?" he asked.

"Oh, I don't know. Something just now made me think of that picture. I always liked it when I was a kid. Something about it. I don't know." My dad hated talking like this. For my father, communication was a matter of practicality, if it did not serve a direct functional purpose, he didn't see the use in talking about it. But he was a little different when I brought this up. His tone, became softer, and he said, "I can make you a copy of it, if you'd like. It's no problem."

My dad was a rough man, but his sensibilities could often be accessed through flattery. That's not what this was about though. I really did think about that picture a lot.

"No that's alright, Dad." I said.

I said no, but would have really liked a copy of it. It was a magnificent photograph. It was a real-life picture of the moon landing, except of course it wasn't quite a real-life picture, it just looked that way. During the first moon landing, while millions of other people around the world gathered around their televisions with their mouths wide open, my dad sat in front of his watching the same live broadcast with an expensive camera and took pictures of the television screen that came out so clear, you would swear the photographs were taken by Neil Armstrong himself. He blew the photograph up and framed it and it hung above our dining room table like a beacon of greatness. But whatever acceptance of conversation my father had through bringing up this family heirloom, dissipated with my curious rejection.

"Is there something else, Drew? It's really late and your mother is not feeling very well."

"Can I just talk to her real quick?"

"She doesn't feel well, Drew."

"Just tell her I want to talk to her, dad."

"Drew, you need to go to bed."

"Whatever, dad. Just put mom on the phone. I didn't want to talk to you anyway."

"You can call her in the morning if you want. Go to bed, Drew. I'm going to hang up the phone now."

"Fuck you, dad. Put her on the goddamn phone."

"First night back and already drunk, Drew. Go to bed."

"Put mom on the goddamn phone!"

"Okay, Drew, I'm gonna tell you this only once: You can do what you want with your life son; your mom and I can't make your decisions for you. If you decide you want to get out of the army then that's fine, but you need to realize that you're not going to be getting those paychecks anymore once you get out. Now I know it can be really rough sometimes, but you have a good thing going right now and it's not the time to just walk away from the kind of pay you're getting. It's not all puppy dogs and rainbows out here either, Drew."

"I just got back fuck's sake. Besides that, how the fuck are you going to suggest I stay in after all this shit? I'm getting out, Dad. Are you fuckin' kidding me? There's no fuckin' way I'm reenlisting. Don't you get that? I'm done. I'm not doing this fuckin' bullshit anymore. I can't. I'm done. I gotta get out and that's fuckin' it."

"And do what exactly? You barely got yourself through high school. You've done well in the army, Drew. You got your sergeant stripes, you said they'd promote you if you reenlisted, on top of the twenty-grand signing bonus they offered; you'd be a fool not to take it. You don't want to see how things are here in the real world; no free meals or guaranteed paychecks out here son."

"The real world? What the fuck do you know about the real world, Dad? *This shit* is the fucking real world. You don't know shit. You never been shot at so what the fuck do you know? You never killed anyone and you're telling me about the fucking real world? Fuck you, Dad."

"Drew. You need to stop yelling. I know this last tour was hard but you need to respect this household. You cannot call here in the middle of the night and yell and swear at your mother or me. Now, I know how hard it must have been. But you're tough. You'll bounce back. You just need a break. And you need to not drink, Drew. It'll take you nowhere. Now, calm down. And you're right, you did just get back, so give yourself a break and see where you're at in a few days when you've had some time to rest and actually think about things clearly."

"Whatever. I can't do it anymore. I'm not going to. I did my four years. I'm done. I've got nothing fucking left. You don't get that."

"I know, son, but you just got back. Give it some time. Things will go back to normal in a couple of weeks. You'll see."

"Yeah, then I'll just leave for another tour."

"That's not going to happen right away, Drew. You know you'll get plenty of time back."

"Fuck *you* plenty of time, Dad. What the fuck do you know? You didn't do shit. You didn't go to fucking 'Nam or anything, so fuck you. Fuck *you!* You hear me, fuck you, Dad. *Fuck you! Fuck you! Fuck you!*"

I didn't hang up. I closed my hand around my phone making as tight a fist as I could and began punching my door with all of my rage. After thrusting back for a third or fourth strike, I could feel the loose and broken pieces falling from my hand as I screamed at no one. My hand bloody and numb with shock, I dropped to my knees and fell to the tile floor in my abandoned apartment. I knew the quiet interrupting knock at my door had to be my downstairs neighbor.

Without getting up or so much as moving my head, I took a deep breath and yelled as loudly as I could, *"No more noise. It's fine. Go the fuck away!"*

I lay exhausted with drunken fury and confused panic expecting another knock that never came. The sobering chore of cleaning my mangled hand had replaced my drunken rage with a bitter emptiness that reminded me just how alone I had become.

CHAPTER SEVEN
End Term of Service

WE HAD BEEN BACK from Iraq for one month and my enlistment in the United States Army was over. A solider is given about four weeks to completely out-process from the military. It's the one task the army gives you more time than is necessary. I guess it's to give you as much time as possible to change your mind and reenlist.

The mood around battalion was always lighter in the direct aftermath of a redeployment, but the nasty air of unbridled testosterone still polluted what should have been a celebrated and grateful return home. Wherever there are insecure men grouped together for a particular job and then separated from all persons without a Y chromosome, the atmosphere takes on a certain archaic familiarity of conflicting patriarchal ideals, reconciling with a blind sense of common duty and circumstantial brotherhood. I couldn't wait to leave it all behind forever.

He called from a distance as he saw me approach, "Hey Hoskins, bout to be up outta this bitch, right?"

Stoker was tall and looked like he should be modeling sweaters in a catalog. He never wore his beret, that way he could show off his always styled and out of regulation light brown hair. Being good looking in the infantry is like being smart in the infantry, it's just a damn waste. He didn't talk like a sweater model though. Stoker was from Detroit and smoked Newport cigarettes.

"Just came from supply, I'm done in this company, man." I said.

"Whatcha gonna do when you get back into the world?"

He reached his closed fist out, dropping it to his side after our knuckles met in the middle.

"Fuck for peace," I said.

"Fuck yeah, bro. Hey man, let me ask you, they fucking you around in your platoon and shit; I bet that asshole Sergeant Hawk's on that ass ain't he?"

Stoker, was privy to the bullshit more than the average paratrooper. He didn't fall under the same organizational guidelines, not being on the line and all, but as I have found, one can almost always become more acquainted with reality by being involved, yet slightly removed, than if one were deep in the midst of the action themselves.

"Yeah man, a little bit. Sergeant Hawk though, he actually hasn't really said shit to me since we got back. It's mostly Sergeant Bastogne and Sergeant Rivera. I don't know, you know how they can be."

"Listen bro, don't listen to what any these motherfuckers tell you. It don't matter what you do when you get out, you hear me? You did your time homie. Grow your hair down to your ass and smoke blunts everyday if that's what you want. It's your life now. Ain't up to them to tell you how to live. They're just too scared to live without somebody telling them what to do all the time."

"Thanks, dude. I appreciate that, man, I do."

I wanted to hug him, but of course didn't. Instead we exchanged crooked half smiles and went on bullshitting.

"Anyway…what's up with you though, you getting outta the arms room ever or what?" I asked.

"Shit man, I don't know. At this point, it's probably just where they'll keep me. I mean, I got less than a year then I'm up outta this bitch myself."

His smile got wider and then went off his face completely and he shook his head toward the ground and then swung it up and said with an exuberance I hadn't seen from anybody since I'd been back,

"These mother fuckers wanna act like it's the only job in the world. Shit, I'll bag groceries, motherfucker, anything's better than this shit."

"That's the way I'm looking at it, man. I mean I wanna go to school and I have some plans and shit, but whatever, dude, I mostly just don't want to do this bullshit anymore. Three tours, man. Three fucking tours. That's it. I'm fucking done."

"Yeah, you got lucky as shit homie. Especially after that last mission. Yo, I heard the LT lost both his legs."

"I don't know man, I think he's still at Walter Reed," I answered.

The platoon made a trip to Washington to see the LT in the hospital just a couple of weeks after we all got back, but I didn't go because I was busy gathering my equipment and clearing and all. The truth of it was that I just didn't want to ever have to see him again. How was I supposed to look at a man who I'd in many ways put in the wheelchair he would forever be bound to? Everybody knew why I didn't really go, but nobody said anything. They all knew he wouldn't want me there anyway.

"And he's gonna be there for a while from what I heard. Just remember homie, that coulda been you."

I knew it could have been me, I'd never forget that. I thought about it that morning and this one and every morning since. A private came down the stairs and entered the room through two shining steel doors. He wore a single stripe on his color, indicating that he'd been assigned to the platoon since we'd been back. His boots were still the same pair issued to him in basic training, the leather rough and dull compared to mine and Stoker's weathered jungle boots. His beret looked puffed up like a baby's blanket instead of a saddlebag like it should have. He stopped in the doorway and Stoker and I looked over at him waiting for him to say something to one of us, we being the only other people in the room. Not knowing that the gesture had nothing to do with his posturing, he snapped to parade rest as soon as my head rose. With shaken words he said, "Um, uh, Sergeant H, The platoon sergeant wants you upstairs in the CP, Sergeant."

"Who the fuck you talking to, Private, that ain't his platoon sergeant anymore. He cleared company; that's your daddy now."

Stoker answered for me and we both laughed and the private looked very nervous and didn't know what to do and said hesitantly, "I don't know, Sergeant, he just sent me down here to find you."

"I gotta get outta here, Stoker, you stay up, man." I said.

"Let me come around there and give you a hug. I may never see you again, homie."

Six months later Stoker was transferred to the line and went with the rest of battalion to Afghanistan. Half his body was blown apart across a dusty road in the east. The rest was shipped back to Fort Bragg in a steel box.

Sergeant First Class Hawk's door was closed which was unusual. I knocked and nobody answered. I put just enough tension on the doorknob to tell that it was unlocked.

"Sergeant Hos," was called out boisterously through the thick pine barrier.

It almost shook with vibration and I felt as though I had been caught doing something wrong.

I cracked the door open just a bit and without looking in I inquired, "Sergeant Hawk?"

A hardened voice grumbled out, "Bring your ass in here, Sergeant Hoskins."

Sergeant Hawk was short, wide, and thick. He wore a five o'clock shadow by nine a.m. His brow line shined with a thin layer of sweat and was all that you saw when he peered in at you with those dim black eyes. He rarely wore his beret and exposed an almost Mohawk thin high and tight haircut. He must have taken a straight razor to the sides of his head at least three times a day. His biceps burst out from his rolled sleeves and his Popeye like forearms rested on his desk like giant tattooed paperweights.

"You clear company yet, Sergeant?" His voice sounded like he'd gargled gravel every morning of his life.

"Roger, just finished up with supply, Sergeant."

My words were stripped of all inflection.

"Your plaque won't be ready before you leave. We'll have to mail it to you when you get to where you're going," he said it without looking up from his desk.

There were papers and manila folders and charts seemingly unorganized all across it.

"Roger, that's all good, Sergeant," I said.

He looked up with one eye and asked, "Where's it that you're from again?"

"Just south of Portland, Sergeant."

"Lot of hippies and faggots out that way."

He stopped what he was doing and stared right at me like he was waiting for me to confirm.

"I guess so, Sergeant."

"You got a job waiting for you back there or something?"

"No, nothing specific, Sergeant."

His nose curled and he turned his head slowly to the left and cracked his neck and looked back down at the papers on his desk and sighed and said, "So what do you got planned when you get out then, Sergeant?"

"I don't know exactly yet, Sergeant. Travel a bit I guess."

I immediately regretted my answer.

"But that's not why you're getting' out though. You can travel in the army, Sergeant Hoskins."

"Roger, Sergeant. But I want to go other places."

"Yeah, like where, Sergeant?"

"Haven't thought about it too much I guess, Sergeant."

He could tell I was nervous and uncomfortable and that's what Sergeant Hawk liked.

"You ain't got one place that you want to go, but you say you're gonna go travel. Not much of a battle plan, Sergeant Hoskins."

His words were picking up a progressively sterner tone.

"Milan, Sergeant. I think I'm going to go to Milan," I said quickly.

"Milan? What is that, China?"

I wanted to tell him that was the real reason I was getting out of the Army, so I wouldn't be some thirty-five-year old asshole who thought Milan was in fucking China.

I answered, "Negative, Sergeant. It's in Italy. My mom's family was from there. My grandmother told me about it when I was a kid."

"Your grandma?" he asked with a sarcastic chuckle.

"Roger, Sergeant."

He leaned back in his chair and raised his chin up so I could see inside his flaring nostrils. I had been under his command for my entire time in the 82nd and he knew exactly how to get under a young sergeant's skin, right where he wanted to be.

"You gonna go to school?"

I wondered how long this examination would continue, and to what end.

"Roger, Sergeant." I said.

"What are you gonna study you think?"

"I was thinking English or maybe journalism. I was good at writing in high school."

"Journalism?" he asked and shook his head back and forth while rolling his eyes in a synchronized motion that drove me mad.

"Roger, Sergeant. Or English maybe." I said.

My tone remained but my pitch got louder.

"Gonna go read books instead of jump out of planes, eh."

"For a while a least, Sergeant."

"How old are you, Hoskins, twenty– two, twenty- three?"

"Twenty- two Sergeant."

"Very young still."

"Roger, Sergeant."

"You gonna use your GI Bill then?"

"Roger Sergeant."

I decided to keep my answers short. He said nothing and looked down at a small stack of papers and began pointlessly moving them around his desk.

"Well Hoskins, I can see that you're as eager as always to get out of here and put the 82nd behind you—"

"It's not just the 82nd, Sergeant."

"At ease, Sergeant."

His tone was abrupt and he had been waiting to jump on me from the moment I walked in.

"Roger," I said and straightened my posture to a more formal stance.

Sgt. Hawk got up from his desk and took his beret off and set it back down. He slowly came around the desk like a shark circling its prey.

Stopping at my side, my eyes still forward and my body locked into parade rest, he brought his tone back a bit and said, "I've watched a lot of soldiers come and go since I been in this man's army and I can tell you that I'm still waiting to hear just one story of a guy who got out and did anything worth talking about. Now I know you think you're going to be that guy. You'll grow your hair and beard. You'll get stoned on some weed, go to college and fuck some girls. And you're a smart guy, Sergeant, and you gotta mouth on you, which will help you out there for a bit. And you're a good-looking kid, so you'll get a bit of pussy too probably. But it won't last more than a year or so and then it'll all be over. You're going to see that college is no place for a battle worn soldier; the world's no place; it's bigger than you think out there and with everything you faced in country, you just ain't gonna want to deal with it all. Take that for what it's worth, Sergeant Hoskins. You were a great soldier. I'm glad you were in my platoon, a good leader. I hope you find whatever it is you're looking for kid."

He put his open hand in front of my eyes and dropped it to my chest. I looked at him from the side and shook it with hesitation.

He squeezed abnormally hard, whether out of affection or disappointment, I don't know.

"Good luck out there, Sergeant." He said.

"Thank you, Sergeant."

He sat down and went back to shuffling around papers.

He looked up from his desk to see I was still there and said, "That's it, you're dismissed, Sergeant."

He was the platoon sergeant and had soldiers to train. I was about to be a peace-loving hair head civilian. That was the last time we ever spoke.

CHAPTER EIGHT
Back But Not Home

CANTRELL THREW A SMALL going away party that was more sad than fun. Never had somebody been so eager and equally regretful to leave something behind as I was leaving the airborne. My one stop flight from Raleigh Durham to PDX left late in the morning. I was anxious...so bad I could feel it in my quivering teeth. It was the first time I'd ever worn my uniform home. I don't know why I did it; maybe something about it being the last time or something. I didn't give two shits about my badges or medals, but after twenty-two months in combat with the 82nd, I had plenty of both. The uniform garnered a special hospitality that I had never enjoyed before or since. My layover was in Houston and it is my sole experience of Texas. Many a derogatory thing can and has been said about the Longhorn State, but the gratitude shown to their infantry veterans can be measured in enough whiskey to intoxicate half the population.

I had a pleasant stay. So pleasant in fact, that what should have been an hour and a half layover ended up as a three hour layover, when I was drunkenly distracted by a proud Texas oil man and two gorgeous young blonde girls who could have been sisters, but were senior roommates at a local college. I took it all in. It felt very strange at first, the more I drank and the more hands I had laid upon my shoulder, the more I felt like there was a reason for where I had been. Most of me knew that there was no reason, not any I could grasp anyway. The beneficiaries of the blood I spilled and watched of my brothers get spilled, were and would always stay untouchable to the people like me. Not just the veterans, to all the people, 'the little people' they call us. The girls, free whiskey, and promise of better things to come kept it all at a safe enough distance to awkwardly enjoy the scene and I don't at all regret embracing the harvest while it was offered.

It would have made things much worse that I came in late, but my mom called my dad while he was out fishing and he was, I'm sure, happy with a few more hours on the river. I flew into Portland well after dark. Being drunk helped at first. I was in good spirits. So much in fact, I had to be helped off the plane by a couple of flight attendants that I cannot remember. It would have been much more embarrassing if I could. The uniform again accounted for my compounded stupor. I was seated across from a middle-aged man and his elderly father who were just coming back from a trip to Washington D.C., and more specifically, the Vietnam War memorial. They liked their whiskey and their soldiers and not wanting to be rude, I shared in the shot and beer they offered me in flight and when we landed I could barely stand up without wavering in my stance.

The gate was crowded as they always somehow are no matter how few people are on a plane. The anxious passengers pushed and jockeyed for position as they all rushed to their common destinations. They took no regard for one another as they grabbed their carry on from above and mean eyed each other from across the aisles with showdowns for the prize of gaining an extra two feet toward the door. I wanted to throw up from all the pushing and the grunting and the unwillingness, and of course the booze.

Soon I was just another desperate traveler pushing my way through the terminal through toddler, cripple, and elder alike, taking no prisoners. I pushed a small, pale, white bald businessman to the side as he blocked the entrance to the bathroom. He nearly dropped his phone as I shoved him aside and he said something low under his breath but I didn't care. The bathroom was brightly lit like they always are and I looked very bad under the fluorescent lights over the mirror. There was strangely nobody at the sinks and I crashed my drunken body into the counter and ran cold water on my hands and cupped it into my face. The uniform looked good, but that's where it ended. My phone rang in my pocket and I saw that it was my mother but I did not answer.

She called again and this time I picked up and said, "Hey mom, just landed, I'll be there in just a few minutes, I gotta go to the bathroom really quickly."

"Are you alright, Drew? You sound..."

"Fine mom, just gotta use the bathroom real quick and I'll be there."

I hung up the phone before she had a chance to respond and threw up in the sink but it was mostly all liquid because I hadn't eaten that day and it went down the drain mostly, except for a few chunks that I had to squish through the drain with my thumb, which made me want to throw up more, but there was nothing left in my stomach so I just dry heaved into the sink for a few moments. My eyes were crimson with drunken strain and I rubbed my face out hard as if I could wipe away the look of pure drunk slop. I washed my hands and face and rinsed my mouth out but only had water so it still tasted awful when I got to my mom and dad. I wondered which they'd smell on me first, the vomit or the liquor.

My parents looked much older than I had remembered them from less than a year before. My mother looked especially tired. But not a sleepy tired. It was the kind of tired that you couldn't get rid of with any amount of sleep. She was a gentle woman who held sentimentality for people she'd never meant. A woman who was infinitely misunderstood by even those closest to her, her strength was her apparent ease at the resilience to be broken by the pain she endured for others.

My father was a cold, but I suppose, good man. He didn't drink and barely swore. He was an inch taller than I was and had the same wavy hair, but where mine was still a dark hazel brown, his had turned a pale gray, as did his beard which was thick but short and always seemed to maintain its exact length. Time had closed one eye just a bit and it appeared slightly smaller than the other, but he was a handsome and still very strong looking man. Once passionate, so I've heard, and a self-described Beat, declaring them to be hippies with philosophy. He was now very tired and spoke nothing of theory but you could still tell that behind his eyes, the same thoughts he had in his youth, boiled with a fiery angst that had since learned to subdue itself for customary presentation.

She would not let me go for well over a minute. As my mother grasped hold of me with both arms, my father and I looked at each other with a subdued smile and shook hands when my mother finally let me go from her desperate loving hug. It was only a short moment before she threw her arms back around me and pulled me into her again like I was still her small child. When she let me go again finally, her face was filled with tears and I wanted to cry with her but did not understand why. She held onto my arm the whole way through the airport and told my father to grab my bag from the conveyer belt so she wouldn't have to let me go again.

"I'm never letting him go ever again," she said and dabbed the still running tears from her cheeks with a tissue.

I wanted to say that I was sorry for yelling on the phone, but couldn't bring myself to raise the issue. Instead I just asked my father how the fishing was and that's what he would have preferred anyway. Our relationship carried, I suppose, no more complication or irregularity than most father-son relationships of the modern, or perhaps any era. We knew each other in a way that didn't show itself often but when it did, it happened in those quietly shared moments where we made each other feel like a real father and son. And those rare occasions had always been enough, at least in his eyes, to show that he loved me.

The city lights paused my breath, the way they glisten off the water makes the river look ablaze with a thousand tiny flames. We lived fifteen minutes south of Portland in a little town called Willamette. You could drive fifteen minutes out of the city in any direction and you'd be right in the middle of nothing but green hills and pine trees. I cannot imagine or more stark contrast to the desert planes of central Iraq.

My mom was completely turned around in her seat for the entire drive. I was an only child and all my grandparents were dead so there wasn't much news, but she told me all about the new puppy she had gotten while I was gone and how she was really excited for us to meet. She told me that my room had been kept the same except for a couple of rock posters that she'd never much liked. My dad asked me what all the new ribbons on my uniform meant and I told him that it was for more of the same. My mom held onto my hand and I fell asleep while she watched me look out the window into the night sky.

CHAPTER NINE
Renovations

MY PARENTS MET AT fifteen and were married at eighteen. They didn't have me until they were almost forty and as a child I was embarrassed about how much older they were than all my friends' parents. My mother was a high-school teacher whose retirement inconveniently coincided with my leaving for the army. Two years after that, my father retired from his air traffic controlling job and had since spent most of his time in his fishing boat.

For the first month back home, I mostly just slept and visited with relatives as they came over one or two at a time. I left the house only to drive to a liquor store to replenish the vodka I stashed in my room. My parents didn't drink and didn't approve of others drinking--which actually made it easier for me at first because neither of them had been around a drunk for so long, I figured they would be none the wiser. I had seen a few of my friends once and it didn't go well, so I hadn't gone back out since. My mom had gotten used to me being home, at least enough to leave without me going with her. I enjoyed her motherly attention. It was quite opposed to anything I had felt for a very long time.

One day they went out and it was too early to sneak vodka sips and I found myself wandering around our property. We had a very big house that my parents bought a few years after my dad got hired by the FAA. The house was two stories and very long from one end to the other. For whatever reason, I went into the garage and found a birdhouse that I didn't remember at first but knew was mine because it had my first name painted on the bottom with '95 written next to it. It was well-constructed. Very sturdy and the corners perfectly flush. The roofing was immaculately done with tiny cedar shingles. My dad had given me a piece of cedar from his collection of random scrap wood and showed me how to split it along the grain when I was young. I didn't know why he had kept it.

I went to the opposite side of the garage where my father kept his many supplies. I will not say the fathers of my generation were better men, that they were tougher, or any of that other bullshit, but they tended to be extremely handy and capable of fixing anything from broken Christmas toys to a lawn-mower engine. My father was no exception and, in fact, epitomized what I thought of as the basic caricature of the overworked grumpy late 20th century father: wise and loving, but too tired and broken to show either.

Along with some paintbrushes, I got out the closest color I imagined the birdhouse used to be. It was late morning but already warm. I filled a tall glass with ice and water and took the supplies outside. The air smelled good, like pine and a bunch of flowers that I didn't know the names of. I laid newspaper down on the grass and took my shoes and socks off and sat down on the ground. Before starting I had a cigarette and listened to the birds with my eyes closed. The sun showed through my thin eyelids and I pushed my face against the inviting beams and enjoyed the warmth. Our house was away from the road enough that you couldn't hear a car no matter how loud the engine was. The only sound was that of the soft late morning breeze pushing through the needles of the massive two hundred foot fir trees that ensconced the entire scene. The Douglas firs had been there long before I was born and were even taller now and would be alive and taller still when I was dead and that thought made me happy.

I painted the house with as much precision as my hand would allow and waited for each section to dry before moving on to the next. I put on three layers of the rich red paint and smoked five or six cigarettes. The freshly coated sides were cool and smooth to touch. The sun was even warmer by then and I closed my eyes again and took off my shirt and rolled the cuffs of my pants halfway up my shins. The grass felt cool and good under my feet and I lay down to feel it against my back. I looked up toward the sky and opened my eyes and thought about all the time I used to spend looking up at the clouds imagining what figures they made in the sky.

My parents came home and brought sandwiches from my favorite deli and a root beer like I used to drink as a kid. We ate the sandwiches outside and my mom commented on how great the birdhouse looked. My father kept eating in silence but I saw him stealing glances at my project with a small smile. We hadn't reconnected in the way I'd hoped yet and I shouldn't even say reconnected, because I was really still looking for an initial connection. A couple of nights before this, he was reading a novel about clandestine military operations and I offered my less than favorable opinion regarding the merit of such missions. But he was unimpressed by my half-drunk diatribe and to be honest, you would have been too. However, it bothered me still. My dad was at least interested enough in the subject to read a fictionalized account about it, but he hadn't asked me a thing about my time in combat since I'd been home.

The sandwiches were good but tasted different than I had remembered them, which seemed to be an increasingly consistent theme since I had come home. My dad sat on a lawn chair in the shade silently while my mom sat on the grass next to me. She talked about all the stuff she still had to do with her flower beds and re-bricking the walkways and such. It all looked perfect to me and anybody else who would have seen it. My dad finished his root beer halfway through his sandwich and went in the house to get another and asked if my mom or I wanted one. We didn't and he didn't come back out until he heard a car pull up driven by my childhood best friend, Kevin.

Kevin was one of only three friends I had kept in close contact with since I had left for the army. Call it a separation of wills. Kevin was different though and I respected him still. He had graduated with a bachelor's degree in history from Oregon State University, which was about two hours south of where we grew up playing baseball and riding bikes together. He was moving back to attend graduate studies at Portland State and we had made plans to move in together when he heard of my divorce.

We all went to school together: him, my ex-wife, and me. They used to date in high school before we ever got together and the truth of the matter was, I stole her from him slowly and quietly under his unsuspecting nose. I didn't try to and certainly never planned to. She had an appeal that other girls our age did not. She looked like a woman when she was fifteen, like she knew how to do things, and did. Kevin had long since forgiven me. I think he forgave me right away. He knew stuff about her that it took me years to figure out. Kevin had also just gotten back into town and, like me, was staying with his parents until we found a place together. We had been talking on the phone but I hadn't seen him yet and I hoped that him being back would make me want to leave the house more.

My mom went over to hug him before I could even get the chance and my father waited and shook his hand like he was his own son. My dad always liked Kevin, I think it's because he fished a lot too. Kevin looked good. We hadn't seen each other in over a year and I panicked a little bit when I thought about how much better he looked than me. His hair was light brown and waved down across his forehead like JFK. He was a terrific looking guy. He always had the right thing to say, especially to parents, that bothered me a lot when we were younger, and still did some. We left my house after a couple of minutes talking to my parents. I was displeased that my father took much more an interest in his scholastic studies than my infantry duties. My father studied history in college too.

We didn't look for an apartment like we told my parents. We went to the bar where I always wanted to drink but was too young to before then. On the way, we talked about unimportant things like what I'd been eating since I'd been back and I was glad that was the content of the conversation. Kevin had always been good at keeping the mood where I needed it to be.

The bar looked just the way I remembered it, painted black, the door and window shutters red. The name was Strega and the atmosphere was like something from a Kerouac novel. Everywhere inside and out were the voices of burgeoning and washed up artists, scholars and professors as well as faux intellectuals and hack poets. The greatest and worst talents of the South Portland Metro congregated in a little house made drinking hole to reconstruct a day when their bohemian lifestyles and artisan pipedreams danced to a softer music. I wanted to be part of it as soon as we walked in. There was no one particular thing about the bar or its crowd that drew me to it. More than anything, I saw something that was as foreign to me before the war as it had been during; that there were no two people who shared a single commonly distinguishable trait. Whether it be the beer guzzling juvenile stupidity of fraternity brotherhood, the locker room culture of dick measuring and ball breaking, or the alpha- male violence of a rape happy military, it is the blind and scared conformity of the many that makes it all possible. Strega had none of that and I knew right away that I wanted to belong to the intimate disconnection.

The bartender asked for Kevin's ID and not mine even though he had a light beard and was quite a bit bigger than me. We got our beers and had a celebratory whiskey shot. Kevin said something short but heartfelt that was moving but I still cannot remember. I felt at home though, like I was supposed to be there with him. After our next drink, everything for me changed very suddenly when I bumped into a man wearing a desert camouflage top like the one I wore in the army. It wasn't much and I didn't at all know what was happening to me or why.

Very, suddenly a scarcity of life came over me like I was right in the middle of a goddamn war zone again. It was all wrong and I knew right away. The feeling I had when my parents and I pulled up to our driveway came back to me and I rushed to the bathroom but did not throw up this time. I splashed water against my face and looked into the mirror. There was a great pressure in my head and stomach and I was sure I was going to have an aneurysm at any moment. Clenching my hair in my fists, I pulled it from my scalp and back away from my eyes, trying to let out all the pressure. I didn't know why I was feeling that way, and didn't know how it was going to stop.

Somebody started to open the bathroom door but I jumped in front of it and pushed it closed immediately and locked it and heard whoever on the other side say, "Hey, man, what the fuck?"

I said, "Sorry, just a minute," through the door but I think he'd already walked away. I went back to the sink and cupped some water into my mouth and looked up at my reflection. I had a little scar on the right side of my face from my first tour in Afghanistan when a bullet connected with a concrete wall and sent debris blasting in all directions. It was not a large scar and could barely be seen unless you knew to look for it. If you did notice it, it looked like I had just cut myself shaving recently or something. It bothered me though and I traced its edge with the blade of my forefinger and felt like crying. Splashing another handful of water onto my face, I dabbed it dry with a paper towel and took a deep breath and walked back out to the bar in hopes that Kevin would act like nothing had happened.

He did and I was very grateful. I think it made it possible for me to stay for a while longer and see if I could maintain. The man wearing the desert cammo top was still in the bar and much older than I but younger than my dad with a long beard and a generally unkempt look. He smiled a lot though and after I saw this, I was better and could sit without my stomach turning over.

Kevin had never wanted me to leave for the army. He wanted me to go to college with him but knew my mind was made up. Something inside me was different from him and the rest of our friends. When I watched those towers burn on TV, I was overwrought with a feeling, not of anger or fear, but opportunity, like everything in my life had somehow set me up to go be a part of what I thought would be historical. And it was. I just didn't end up on the side of history I had wanted.

It felt better outside. Like I had somewhere to escape if I had to. We sat down at one of three tables on the large awning covered front porch. It faced the street and it was busy with traffic and pedestrians. It wasn't a loud or restless busy though. The street carried on a quiet life to itself, as if the passing cars and people were its flowing blood.

Kevin wanted to tell me about school. But not about his school; he was excited for me to go to school.

"It's not that hard," he said. "It's a lot like the army I'm sure. Easier I mean, but like you always said about basic training and infantry school and everything, it's a lot easier than people make it out to be. It's like anything else, the people who try it and fail want to make it sound like it was this nearly impossible task, you know, it gives 'em an excuse to fail and all. And the people who do finish act the same way, like it was all super hard and stuff, because they want you to think they did something special. It's all nonsense though. It's as hard as you want it to be. I would just say to major in something you're actually interested in. It's not even worth it otherwise," he said.

"My dad says not to major in English or anything like that, cause I won't be able to get a job with it or anything."

"Yeah, whatever. I mean, that's true and all, but it's not like any of these other degrees really offer you much more."

"Yeah, I just already spent four years learning one skill that didn't do shit for me. I really don't want to do that all over again."

"You know, I still have some of the stories you and Roger wrote in AP English. Oh yeah, and that sketch you two did too; I found a bunch of that stuff the other day. You remember that thing?" he asked and laughed, spilling beer over the top of his glass.

"Yeah, I remember that. That fucking thing. What did we call it?"

"*Here is Our Youth*. I still got it. No, that thing was hilarious, everybody remembers that. For real, you should. Yeah, do English.

That's definitely you're thing. You know, you need to hit up Roger when he gets back. He's trying to publish a book of short stories or poetry or something like that. I know he'd like to get together on something with you."

"*Back?* Where'd he go?"

"He went to South America, backpacking and stuff I guess."

"I thought he was growing or something?"

"Yeah, he is, but you know how he is; he'll just pick up and go whenever and you don't know when he's coming back."

"Fucking bastard. I shoulda done that when I got out instead."

But I never actually would have and it made me a little sad when I thought about it.

"Nah, you're gonna like college, trust me."

"Fuck, I hope so. It can't be worse than what I'm used to at least."

"No. You're going to like it. It's perfect for you."

"I'm actually kind of excited to start reading regularly again. You know I've been going through some of my mom and dad's old books from college since I've been back. I re-read *The Old Man and the Sea* the other day. My dad gave it to me a long time ago, when I was about thirteen I think. He told me I should read it and learn it now; that I'd be a lot better off when I turned his age. I didn't know what the hell he meant, but I did read it. Rereading it though the other day, I think I actually get it now; I think I get what he meant, you know. Fucking Hemingway, man, writes just like my old man talks, when he actually does decide to talk. I think that's why he always liked him so much. It's probably why I always liked him too. It kinda replaced having a dad who wanted to talk to me," I said.

Kevin put his beer down and his everlasting smile got a bit smaller and he said to me, "Your dad's a lot better guy than you give him credit for. I know he's always been kind of hard on you, but he's not that bad really."

It put me off, hearing somebody defend him. But the prob-

lem was that he was right, as far as he knew. My dad was too emo-
tionless to be cruel, especially with people around. He never yelled or
belittled me in front of my friends; he never said anything bad about
me really. It wasn't what he said to me though, it's what he didn't
say. And realizing that Kevin didn't understand that, I became a little
angry with him and my tone was a bit caustic because of it.

"No, I know my dad's not a bad guy. He's never done anything for me to say otherwise. But that's not all it is, you know? Being a good dad means more than not hitting your kid. I mean that's
pretty easy, not running out on your wife or beating your kids or anything. He never got drunk and did anything to my mom or me. I've
never even seen my dad drink, I guess--either of my parents. Maybe
they should have though, they'd have been in a better mood sometimes," I said and took a big gulp of my cold beer.

"You remember my dad at all?"

Kevin's dad died of liver cancer right before we graduated
high school.

"Yeah, man. Of course I do," I said.

"Remember how he'd always take us to the Mariner games
whenever he had business trips over the weekend in Seattle?"

Kevin's smile hadn't come back to his face yet. I knew he
missed his dad a lot, because after he died, Kevin never talked about
him at all.

"Yeah, man. That was so awesome. We'd do the same thing
every time. A sandwich and chowder at Pike Street, then to the King-
dome for the ballgame. Shit, man, remember how cool it was when
Safeco Field finally opened?"

Kevin just nodded his head and smiled a bit and let me continue talking.

"I miss those days, man. We felt so grown up, because he'd
drop us off at the game by ourselves while he went and did stuff for
work. See, that's the thing, man, your dad didn't like baseball and
sports and stuff either, he may not have gone and sat there with us,
but he took at least took us. He took you to do stuff that *you* wanted

to do. That's what dads are supposed to do. My dad never took us to any games. Your dad was awesome though, we'd eat and watch the game, then he'd pick us up and we'd get more food and go home."

Kevin nodded in that obligatory manner and I could tell he was only waiting for me to finish talking.

"Do you remember what my dad did for a living?" he asked with stiff lips.

"Yeah, man, he worked for Gerber Blades. So did my grandma way back in the day. Best fucking knives on the planet, man. Everybody in the army uses 'em," I said.

"Yeah, that's right, Gerber Blades. He went up to Seattle to meet with other distributors," he said with a curious tone.

"Yeah. And we'd watch the game," I said and Kevin smiled at me like I had spent my whole life thinking the earth was flat.

"My dad didn't drop us off to meet with business partners. That's what he made it look all right, and that's what he told my mom he was doing. But really, he was meeting with a woman he had been sleeping with since just after my parents got married. For some reason, he told my mom right before he died. But I always knew."

He grabbed our empty glasses and without saying anything else, he walked inside to get us another beer.

CHAPTER TEN
Out on the Weekend

MOST OF THE PEOPLE I had served with were either still in the army or dead. Robertson got out a year before me. We had come up together. He had signed up for three years and moved back to Michigan. Last I knew, he was working part-time at a local grocery store and battling the VA over his disability claim. They told Robertson there was nothing really wrong with him. They said what was wrong with him didn't have anything to do with combat. They offered him bi-monthly group therapy and a guided trip to Lake Superior with a bus full of other battle fatigued young men. Like most of us, Robertson opted for the bottle. It served him well while he was in and it proved to be his only steady companion when he got out. I would have never talked to him again if things had gone better. His cell phone had been disconnected, but I had his home number too.

His mother answered. We'd never met, but we'd talked many times over the years. She was the type that made you forget she wasn't your own mother. Her voice sounded like she should be making five layer cakes on a cable network's cooking program. She was all mid-west.

"Oh Drew, hello. It's so good to hear from you. Oh my, Chris told me you'd come back. And how are you darling?"

"Good. Good. I'm good. How are you?"

"Oh, you know I'm always fine; it's you boys I worry about. Chris told me how hard it was for you all this time."

"Nothing he wouldn't have been able to handle."

"I'll tell him you said that. It would make him feel good I think. It was really hard for him while you boys were over there this time. I think he wanted to be there with you."

"We could have used him a few times, that's for sure."

"He talked about it every day. We all worried. He couldn't find out much. When you boys were in Haditha toward the beginning, it was on the news all the time, but not much after that."

"Yeah, we lost eight guys that first night. My dad said it was all over CNN."

"We were just sick. And nobody knew who had died. Everybody was sure it was their son or husband or friend. Did you know any of them?"

"I knew six of them. The other two were privates like Robertson and me when we first went to Afghanistan. They didn't even know anything yet."

"It just makes me sick to my stomach."

"Yeah, it's over for me though, finally."

"And none happier than your parents I'm sure."

"Yeah."

"Well listen Drew, I don't want to keep you because I know Chris will want to talk to you. I just have to go up to his room and get him. He stays up 'til three or four in the morning. He still has trouble sleeping. Hold on just a second, hun, I'm just going to knock on his door."

I heard the cautious sound of a single knuckle tapping the wooden door, followed by a soft maternal voice saying, "Chris, sweetie, it's Drew on the phone for you."

I heard the door open quickly and Robertson breathing heavily on the other end. "Okay Drew, you call back real soon and send me your new address, so I can send you some cookies."

"Thanks Mrs. Robertson I will, I sure missed them this time."

"Bye Hun."

"Talk to you later."

A roaring cough followed by a hacking and low grumble whisked into the receiver and Robertson said, "Hoskins, buddy, how you doing?"

"Made it man."

"Goddamn, buddy. Good to fucking hear from you. I lost all my numbers a while back when my stupid phone broke so I couldn't give anybody a call or nothing."

"Yeah man, I tried calling you but the number was disconnected. Then I finally remembered that I still had your Mom's number in my old phone from when you called her at Myrtle Beach that one time."

"Fuck yeah buddy, nice. I'd never remembered that."

"Smarter than the average bear, my boy."

"You and fucking Browning yeah, with your fucking books and shit. Fucking Browning. Fuck. I can't believe he's gone." He breathed heavily into the phone again and it made that staticky sound and he added after a moment, "I miss you buddy."

"Yeah, me too. But fuck all that shit man, how are *you*?"

"Shitty."

"What. Really, what's up?"

"Nothing."

"No really man, what's up?"

"Nothing, really. Just how things are."

"How things are?"

"Yeah, I don't want to bum you out. You're just getting out. You need to have a good fucking time. Like you and me and Cruise and Browning all used to. Like we did at Myrtle, you know."

"Yeah, but what is it man? The VA still fucking you around?"

"Oh fuck yeah buddy. But I don't even worry about that shit anymore. I just need to get a fucking job."

"I thought you had one. Weren't you working the stock room at some grocery store?"

"Got fired."

"What? You? Why, for what?"

"Boss thought I was drinking. Smelled booze on me."

"Smelled booze on you?"

"Yeah, it was from the night before. Told him I wasn't drinking during work, but he didn't believe me."

"What the fuck man? Shit man we used to stink of last night's booze till two in the afternoon when we were in the eighty deuce."

"That's what I told him. He didn't give a fuck. Fired me on the spot. Couldn't get unemployment either. Got my fucking mom taking care of me and shit. How's that for fucking making it on the outside, eh?"

"Oh man, that shit's not your fault, dude. That guy's just an asshole; no fucking respect obviously. The shit we had to fucking do; motherfuckers just don't know."

"They'd fucking shit themselves if they had to live a single day of it."

"Fucking-A right man."

"Well, what are you planning on doing now, buddy?"

"I don't know man, I'm going to go to school I guess. Use my GI bill. You think of trying that out at all?"

"College? Fuck that. I can't be sitting in some square goddamn room with some jerk off fucking teacher telling me what I should know."

"Yeah, I feel you on that, man."

"You'll do good though. You were always kinda nerdy."

"Yeah?"

"For a paratrooper, you were."

"Yeah, I suppose."

"I'm just glad you made it home."

"Shit, me too. I should probably get going though, man."

"Yeah, me too. But give me your number real quick, so I got it though."

"Oh yeah dude, you got paper?"

"Send it buddy."

It was a familiar voice. A common voice. I hadn't heard it for almost a year, but it didn't matter. I think we were both a little better from the talk. On my end, at least it was enough optimism to push me out the door and into the sphere of social normality. Leaving the house had been hard since being back and I know both my mom and dad were looking for me to make some kind of move. The weather and beautiful summer scenery played their parts. Northwest summers are like something out of old pastoral poems. Everything is green and smells alive and all the wild animals come out and their songs and dances can be watched and heard at all hours by attentive eyes and ears. On this night though, I was listening to the calls of those other wild animals, the kind that dwell in the cities and drive cars and eat out of plastic containers. As Robertson had already learned, there is a savagery in war that has its unfortunate recollections in all aspects of life. After just two months back in the world, I had seen that wherever people gather under the guise of community for the sake of the mass production of needless goods, the stench can be every bit as great, and the sounds just as screechingly awful to the senses of the willfully optimistic. Until school started in the fall, I would have no schedule, nowhere to be and nothing I had to do, nothing but thinking and drinking.

Kevin and I and some friends of ours from high school that I didn't talk to anymore went on one of the summer's last wine walks. Wine walks were city-sponsored events involving over thirty bars and local businesses. For twenty dollars, sex desperate boys, sparsely clad college girls, young professionals, and middle- aged yuppies paid twenty dollars for a glass and a map of the involved business establishments. Each place you traveled would pour a small amount of cheap wine in your wine walk designated glass. Participants could drink as much as they could partake from two to five o'clock. Kevin and the rest of our indistinguishable friends went every month. It was our slow pace that bothered me at first. But it's what eventually led me right to her.

Along with Kevin, there were our other friends, Jason, Brian, Justin, Steve, and Matt. We looked stupid together walking down the street from bar to bar. I always took notice of groups of young 'men' like ours and was embarrassed to be part of it but thought 'fitting in' would put my mind more at rest than it had been. I also knew that if I wanted to meet a girl, my best chance was to be in the socially comfortable midst of other people who looked and dressed almost exactly the same. There was a kind of herd mentality that took over during events like those. For whatever reason, girls like the ones we all wanted to sleep with were more receptive to a guy who had a surrounding group of other guys who were practically indistinguishable in both appearance and character.

As our group walked along the city streets, I became increasingly disgusted by my approach. Every place looked the same. They all had over confident twenty somethings with emaciated arms and wrist tattoos and misplaced facial piercings; they knew nothing about the liquor they poured or the music they played. The patrons were their polar opposites, dumbbell pumping, cheap beer drinking, polo-shirt wearing frat boys looking for a girl drunk enough to make a bad decision.

We were at our fourth bar and hadn't had enough to be drunk.

Justin said to me in a concerned voice, "Hey, Drew, you feeling alright, man?"

Everybody else tried to ignore me. I walked five steps back from the group after the second bar. At the last place, I didn't even go in and instead waited outside smoking and took Justin's glass of wine as he came out for a cigarette. He wasn't at all upset that I took his quarter glass of boxed wine. But I was angered that he said anything to me at all. None of it was for me. The wine, the crowd, the loud bullshit music, I just wanted to drink.

Instead of standing outside with a scowl and a cigarette, I went into the next place but, skipped the line for wine and went right to the bar and ordered a shot of whiskey. Kevin came up beside me but didn't say anything and I ordered himself one too.

"Make that two over here." I said to the bartender as he poured the first shot.

"To the summer," Kevin said and I brought my glass up to his and together we brought them down to the bar, tapping the bottom of the glasses lightly on the surface and taking them down.

"Let's do another," I said.

"That's probably good for now. It's going to be a long day. We need to pace ourselves," he said.

"Fuck that." I said and waved over to the bartender and called out, *"Two more, we want two more right over here."*

"We really shouldn't. They catch up to you by the end of this thing. I'm telling you, it's going to be a really long day."

Kevin motioned over to the bartender that we were good and I grabbed his hand awkwardly and set in on the bar, pressing it down under my hand.

"Drew, we don't need another shot right now. I'm telling you, just wait 'til later. Let's just go."

"Go get in fucking line for your bitch wine if that's what you want to do, Kevin. I'm getting another shot."

He said nothing and walked away and got in line with the rest of our friends.

"Make that *one* shot," I said to the bartender.

But he didn't pour any shots. He told me I couldn't drink there anymore, to come back another time.

"Just pour me another fucking shot, dude."

"No," he said and with that I slammed my glass down and broke it on the bar top and his reserved hospitality escaped and he told me with a waving fist and loud screams to *"Get the fuck out!"* And, *"Don't ever come back here!"*

It made a little stir and I faded into the crowd and out the door, not wanting my friends to see me as the source of the commotion.

Once out the door, I ripped off my twenty-one and over bracelet and walked down the road toward Strega with my head forward and eyes up, panning back and forth like I was going through the streets of Iraq. At that moment and many moments since I'd been back, I wanted to be in Iraq. Not in the army anymore, I was glad I was out, but combat was something that becomes a part of you, and for however long a soldier lives, they will carry that part with them with a varying degree of comfortable ease or violent hostility. Strega did not participate in wine walks. Saturdays were open mic nights there. I didn't like poetry much and thought about going somewhere else when I read the sign outside, but went in because it wasn't at all busy and I didn't want to be around many people.

I shot a glass of whiskey and ordered an Indian Pale Ale. Nobody was on stage yet and I asked the bartender when the performances were going to begin, because I actually wanted to see somebody as vulnerable as I felt. There was never a question as to whether I had made the right decision by leaving the military. It was a place that taught me much and I was grateful to be a part of, but was completely through with. It was this fact that was the source of my torment. I knew I was done, that I no longer had a place where I had once thought of as the only refuge of a real man. I didn't know if I was that real man, or if I even wanted to be, or if that was something that was even ever real. Identity can be everything, and losing the brand we wear as soldiers can be a devastating shock to the psyche of the vulnerably sentimental.

Shitty thoughts were interrupted by the sound of a delicate index finger gently tapping a microphone, followed by a beautiful woman saying, "Hi, I'm Hadley Landon, can you guys hear me alright?"

The voice was soft and innocent, but had an air of confident wisdom in its delivery. It made me think of stories my mom used to tell me about Joan Baez shows in the late 60's. Her faded blue jeans sat low on her hips and her legs were strong looking at the top; she wore no socks in an old pair of tan moccasins. Her shape was something reserved for comic book heroines. The stage was lit only by the sunlight that shined through the open front door and two windows. Thick blue curtains that were tattered at the edges and corners hung on each side and looked like they had not been closed since the place opened, but they contributed to whatever kind of ambiance it was that they were trying to achieve. I would describe it as the hypothetical drinking hole of the even more hypothetical child of Zelda Fitzgerald and Oscar Wilde. And there was this young beautiful proud but alone poet, Hadley Landon, standing in the middle of it all. Her cheeks were full and sat high on her face and her eyes were big and a light green that looked almost blue at a distance. She wore her hair long and it fell haphazardly in loose elegant curls down past her strong, but feminine shoulder line.

Her small smile faded as she pulled out a piece of paper. Looking at it for only a couple of seconds, she let it drop gently to the floor and leaned into the microphone with almost closed eyes and read her words.

I want to be someone new. Not you. Not me. Not my mom or Marilyn Monroe or Mother Teresa. I want to be those two spots of dust on that motionless ceiling fan in the old abandoned plastic factory on 4th. We want to be nothing but we are and we'll keep punching the clock and pulling the chains and tugging the nerves and biting with our tired teeth and rusted jaws till they all snap or break or dissolve into dust and fall and break apart. I can't see the stars because they just aren't there. And the sky is all black too because we turned it black. And where's the old white bearded man in the sky who we all forgot about with the neighbors while we watched fireworks and ate pieces of animal flesh between toasted bread with sesame seeds while all the other seeds dried up and sank back into the earth where we all come from? Where did he go? He's here in the room with us now and he has no place else to go either.

She bent over and picked up the paper and a few people clapped and she walked off the stage. Her words were strong and I wanted more. That was bravery. She was strength. She was salvation. A shaded summer Arcadia for me and whoever was listening. This was a woman. This was a human being. She was unsure but unafraid. She was an explorer, a pioneer, an astronaut. Without ever knowing it, she was the real reason I fought to live through that ambush. She was Hadley Landon and I had never seen another human being like her before in my life.

When I worked up the nerve to talk to her, my words were not fluid like they were in my head while her presence still radiated my thinking. I stumbled but she made it easy. She smiled and her mouth, which was before perked to a heart shaped flower, went wide and her teeth shined perfectly between full pink lips. Everything escaped, my words: the war, all wars. I wanted to say something but I wanted the moment to last forever.

Instead, I said, "Hi, I really liked your poem."

"Thank you so much. I was really nervous, I just wrote that one a couple of days ago."

Her voice was just like it was on stage. Soft and comforting but projecting out as if she were speaking to everyone on earth. I doubt she even needed the microphone.

"Oh, it was great." I wished I had something more to say about it but didn't know thing one about poetry and thought it better not to reveal that bytrying to sound like I did.

"And what was your name?"

"Drew."

"Hi, I'm Hadley."

We shook hands and my body melted and my knees became weak and I knew I had to do something so I asked, "You want to get a beer or something?"

"Yeah, sure. I was on my way over there anyway."

It was a short few steps to the bar but I let her walk ahead of me and raised my hand to the bartender to get his attention. "Whatever she wants and another IPA please."

"Oh, that's fine, I already have a tab open."

"You sure, it's no problem?"

"Yeah, they probably won't even charge me for that one. I'm here every week."

"You come for the poetry readings?"

"Yeah, every Saturday. I don't remember seeing you here before though. First time?"

"It is."

"Well, I really hope you come again."

She said the words like she had meant them and my chest tightened and my breath shortened.

"Oh yeah, the readings don't usually start 'till later on. With the wine walk and everything, they started early this week," she added with her hands in her back pockets and rocking slightly back and forward at the hips.

There was a nervous way to her eager movements that women conceal much better than men. I can't even imagine what kind of a train wreck of a nervous patient I must have come off as; Hadley went about like I was James Bond or something though and I hadn't been made to feel that way in a very long time.

"I think I will. Yeah, maybe next week," I quickly answered.

I knew though that I would definitely be back next week.

"Good. That makes me happy. I hope you come. Do you read much poetry?"

"Not as much as I'd like to, yeah, not much really at all. But I do like it a lot. I read novels more I guess. I've always just read books more, but yeah, I really want to start reading more poetry I think."

"There's nothing else like it. It's so much more precise than any book can be, so direct, right to the soul, all the extra stuff just cut away. All blood and bone. Not even music can touch you like a poem. Nothing can ever be so pure. There's no truer language."

I was completely taken. I wanted to say more. Ask her more, but no amount of whiskey would have made it possible for me to do more than I was doing. My courage extended only so far as to speak with her at a base level. It wasn't just her physical beauty, plentiful as that was. It was her aura. Cautious as I am to use the word, that is what she had; her own aura. Perhaps her most rare quality was that she carried a casual confidence in herself and everything she said while at the same time exuding an innocent optimism toward every person that came in her presence. Without effort, she acquainted me immediately with exactly everything I had always hoped existed in the world. I can't imagine that any man could sit down with her for more than one minute without falling hopelessly in love.

CHAPTER ELEVEN
Like a Tic

MANY THINGS CAN BE attributed to my answering the phone call. Thoughts and anticipations of Hadley had pushed her to the side for the last week, but she was the last woman I had been with and the only one, for however superficial the origin may have been, that I had ever been in love with. More than anything though, it was that she was a part of a past that I wanted desperately to let go forever. My mother always told me she'd come back though and while her phone call didn't quite qualify as such, we would have our inevitable reconnection.

"Hi Drew. It's been a long time."

I said nothing at first. I breathed into the phone deliberately and took a deep and emphasized breath like I was going to say something extensive and then slowly uttered, "Yes, it has."

"What are you doing? Are you back in Oregon?"

"Yeah. I moved back right after I got out."

"Are you living with your parents?"

"Right now, but Kevin and I are getting a place downtown soon. Why?"

"How is Kevin?"

"He's fine. He graduated. Where are you?"

"I'm in North Carolina."

"Still? You stayed there?"

"Why wouldn't I?"

"Why would you? You're not from there."

"I didn't want to move back home."

"So, you've met somebody already then?"

"Drew, I didn't call to fight with you."

"Why did you call?"

"To see how you were doing; if you were okay. I loved you for a long time, Drew. I can't just pretend like I never knew you."

"Why not? I am."

"You don't ever think about me anymore?"

"I still do. I'm trying not to though."

"Does it make you sad thinking about me?"

"No, it puts a wide fucking smile on my face, Sarah. What do you think?"

"Don't be like that, Drew. I just wanted to see how you were doing and I miss talking to you sometimes."

"Maybe you shouldn't have divorced me then, Sarah."

"That's not what it was about, Drew."

"Okay. What was it about then?"

She took a long breath and held it. When she let it out, her throat made a soft whistling sound and I remembered how she used to do that when she was nervous and it made me angry that she was doing it now.

"I was just really scared, Drew."

"Of what?"

"Of lots of things."

"What the fuck did you have to be scared of? It was my ass getting shot at every day."

"You don't think that scared me?"

"Probably did. But that's not why you left."

"No. That's not why I left," she said in a hesitated agreement.

"Then why? What were you afraid of?"

"Of you, Drew. I was afraid of you."

"Of me? You thought I'd hurt you?"

"No. I knew that you wouldn't. Well, when I think about it now I know that you wouldn't. It just got to be too much. It was just constant."

"What was constant?"

"The pressure."

"For you?"

"No, Drew. For you. But I'm the one you lived with. I'm the one you came home to when you were pissed off about your platoon sergeant. I'm the one who slept next to you every night when you'd wake up in the middle of the night ready to kill whoever you thought was attacking you."

"I'm really sorry you had to go through all that, Sarah."

"Drew, don't be an asshole about this."

"Me don't be an asshole? You're calling me up and asking me how I'm fucking doing and then you say you miss me and tell me the only reason you left was because, why, it just got too scary for *you?* Get the fuck outta here, Sarah."

"I just wanted to see how you were doing and tell you that I'm really sorry."

"You're really sorry. That's great, Sarah. Is there anything else you just have to tell me? Because if there isn't, I think I'm going to get back to doing anything else right now."

"It's fine. I don't expect you to want to talk to me."

But I did. I was angry, and very hurt and talking to her reminded me of the love I was trying to forget about, but I still wanted to keep talking to her. Regardless of what I said or how I acted, I still missed her, and was mostly angry that she reminded me of that. We talked for another twenty minutes or so, until the conversation got too sour and she got off the phone, not hanging up, but I'm sure just one comment away from it.

Unbeknownst to her, and even myself at the time, my ex-wife had granted me a favor that is rarely yielded from a former lover. We had spoken long enough for me to remember how boring she was and it became at that moment more obvious to me than it ever had before, just why I had married the girl who used to give me erections while I watched her jump up and down in her cheerleading uniform when we were both still in high school.

CHAPTER TWELVE
A Good Day

IN TELLING KEVIN OF the conversation I had with my ex-wife, Sarah, I was reacquainted with the guilt I once felt for taking her from him years ago. However, that guilt did not extend so far that I reserved the conversation from Kevin's still misplaced heart, and I curiously replaced the guilt with the gesture of inviting him to come see the girl I was now enchanted by.

Kevin picked me up at my parent's house and we smoked a half a joint on the way downtown. We talked about school after I was done verbally daydreaming of Hadley. I got a text message on the way:

[555-6480]

Hey Buddy its Robertson. Got a new phone. One of those pay as you go kind… ha ha, but whatever. It was good talking to you the other day. Call any time.

[555-0506]

Glad you got a cell. Good talking to you too man. I'll hit you up here again soon. Tell your mom I said hi.

[555-6480]

Will do. Send your address there too buddy. She's been baking your cookies since early this morning.

[555-0506]

7278 Lakeshire Ct. Willamette, Oregon 97041

Kevin asked who I was texting but I didn't say anything and just told him how cool it was at Strega the other night. We arrived at the bar a bit late and the first two poets had already performed. I spotted Hadley mixed in with a group of other girls who all but disappeared in the energy and beauty that she occupied around them.

The bar was crowded and the line to get a drink was at least five deep so I went outside to have a cigarette on the front porch where I could still look in through the open door and see Hadley leaned against the back wall listening attentively to whoever was on stage. I didn't care who was onstage. I was there to see her. Kevin talked about something that I can't remember because I was too distracted by Hadley.

His words slowed eventually until he fell silent and I finally said to him. "She's here. That's her right in there, man. Between that tall girl with the Medusa tattoo on her arm and the hipster with the Rolling Stones t-shirt."

"Yeah, she's pretty. Really nice hair."

His attention was on the Hipster and not Hadley; Kevin liked girls who spent a lot of time trying to look like they didn't spend any time getting ready.

"I'm going to go wait in line. I want a drink. You want me to just get you something?" Kevin asked.

"Yeah. Thanks man, just get me an IPA." I said without taking my eyes off Hadley.

Kevin came back with our beers excited that Hadley had friends there for him to talk to. He had a thing for girls with tattoos even though he, of course, had none.

Hadley handed her half full beer to the girl Kevin was eyeing and walked up to the stage slowly, but deliberately, and I held my breath until she spoke into the microphone.

"Hi, everybody. Thanks for coming. My name's Hadley Landon. I wrote this one this morning. It's called 'Known'"

We all just want to be known
Known to somebody
Known to everybody
Known to the world
Known to the trees
Known to the wind
And to the grass
And to the volcanoes and to the sun and the stars
Forgotten as we feel
Alone as we are
There is another place where we can be seen and touched the way we were when we were still pure
That place is here and now and we are all part of the same great dream

She smiled a little bit, just to herself, and without looking at the audience. She nodded her head politely and walked gracefully from the stage. The room clapped delicately.

Kevin leaned over to me and said, "That was cool, I guess. You should go get her a drink. Here." He took my beer from my unsuspecting hand and finished it in one drink and said, "There you go. Now go stand in line with her."

I hadn't left the house since I'd seen her the week before and the stimulation of the crowd closed in on me a bit but I pushed through and approached her as she leaned against the bar.

"Hi. Drew. right?"

My heart stopped in my chest and my face swelled with nervous excitement that she had remembered my name.

"Yeah, yeah, Drew, that's right. And you're Hadley."

"You remembered. Nobody ever remembers. They usually call me Haley the first five times we talk."

Idiots! I thought to myself. And said, "Of course. Yeah Hemingway's first wife was named Hadley. It's the only other time I've heard the name, but I always thought it was such a great name."

"You like Hemingway?"

"I do. A lot, actually."

"Have you read *A Farewell to Arms?*"

"It's probably my favorite. You remind me of Catherine from that book. How he describes her I mean."

"You know that she was based off his wife, Hadley?"

"I wondered about that maybe."

"He always regretted what had happened with them. I think she was the only woman he ever really loved. It's why he created a character based on her and then had her tragically die; he had to replace what really happened in his head with what he could live with a little better."

"What can I get you?" The bartender interrupted.

I leaned just over Hadley's shoulder. I became weak just smelling her hair. It was like an unknown sweet fruit that my senses had never before known.

I wanted to introduce her to Kevin but noticed that he was already at a table with Hadley's friends as we walked from the bar with our matching IPAs. He was sitting between the girl with the Medusa tattoo and the hipster with the Rolling Stone t-shirt, but facing and talking only with Medusa. Both girls were good looking and had it not been for Hadley, I would have been thrilled to be in either's proximity, but as it was, their appeal was diminished to nothing. Hadley and I were coming up to the table.

I quietly said to her with hints of embarrassment, "This is my friend, Kevin."

He was not at all an unwelcome guest at the table though, which became readily apparent as soon as we sat down with them.

It was a small, circular wooden table, painted black. It was against the wall opposite the stage, about in the middle of the bar. There was a bench on the side against the wall and a painting of a nude Statue of Liberty holding a Glamour magazine instead of a torch that hung on the wall above it. Kevin and the two girls sat on the bench and Hadley and I took seats at two chairs on the other side of the table facing away from the stage.

There was a break in the performances and the bartender put old jazz on quietly It felt like we were in the middle of a 1920s novel. I didn't know anything about jazz at the time, other than I liked the way it sounded and it made me feel like I was in a part of time that would have favored me more than the one I was in. It's a horrible shame that so few people can indulge in feelings of nostalgia for times they were never a part of. It must be terrible to be restricted in feeling joy for only one's own limited experiences. Most of us at the table were part of that terrible disposition. Hadley most certainly was not. She sat in an engaged silence. Her body and smile told you that she was right where she wanted to be while her minded wandered in the imaginations of another life.

Kevin introduced me to everybody including Hadley and I introduced Hadley to Kevin and they shook hands.

Kevin said, "Hey, it's really nice to meet you."

Things were good and I remember being in war and hoping that someday I'd get to be a part of something like what was happening.

Hadley asked me how Kevin and I had met.

"We grew up together. We're both from here and I just got out of the army actually and just moved back. We're getting a place together here soon."

"You were in the army?"

"Yeah, I did four years."

"Did you go overseas?"

"Three times. Once to Afghanistan and twice to Iraq. Just got back from Iraq a few months ago actually."

"Oh, my God. I'm sorry, I just mean…I don't know; I guess I just never have talked to anybody our age that was in the war. I guess I still just think of veterans as being old guys like my grandpa. Not that I mean anything like…"

"It's okay," I said quickly trying to relieve her of the embarrassment I could tell she was feeling. I understood her reaction though. It still surprised even me at times.

"Well, I'm really glad you're back and that you're okay," she said.

"Yeah, thanks. I got kind of lucky, I guess," I said.

"I think anybody who comes back is lucky," she said and took a drink of her beer.

I thought of the LT and how he came back, but was not very lucky. I was lucky. I hurt. I had guilt and I'd always have both. But my scars were mostly on the inside and whatever you might think about that being worse than the ones on the outside. Know this, *all* soldiers wear scars on the inside; it is the ones on the outside, the missing limbs, the missing ears and noses, and the burned off faces that people see and that you have to look at yourself. Those are the ones that make those inside wounds nearly impossible to reconcile. But except for a couple of scars that I could have gotten fighting in the playground or playing high school football, I looked untouched. And while that is again only half, it is a lucky and important half. I hadn't thought about things in this way until Hadley said that to me. Without her ever knowing or even trying, she was healing me better than I could have ever done on my own. And it was for this reason, perhaps more than any other, that I loved her instantly.

CHAPTER THIRTEEN
Sunday Breakfast

KEVIN GOT THE NUMBER of the girl with the Medusa tattoo. They went out the next night but nothing happened. I told Hadley that I'd see her next week. The hipster left by herself long before any of this. Kevin told me that it was a mistake not to have gotten Hadley's number but I knew I'd see her again next week and I had thought it better to wait. Our conversations were great and ranged from literature to local beers. Hadley knew much more about both but didn't make me feel at all inadequate. There was something that happened when we were together, just listening to her voice, her ideas, it felt as though I was being reacquainted with a humanity I had since forgotten.

She learned that I was in the army and I learned that she was from Ohio. She had grown up in Cincinnati, moved for college and decided to stay. I couldn't imagine her in a place like Ohio. The curious trend for young independents congregating to the west coast had diminished from where it was in my parents' young adulthood. But there still existed, and I pray always will, a tendency for the bright and open minds of America's youth to head toward that bright blue hopeful glow of the Pacific Ocean.

The following day was a Sunday. Not at all a day of rest in the Hoskin's house. As I said before, my parents were not at all religious. My father's religion was hard work and my mother's too. Before I began high school, I can scarcely remember a single Sunday that was not spent working in some manner on one of our eight perfectly manicured acres. Whether it was collecting leaves in the fall, windblown tree branches and limbs in the winter, replanting in the spring, or watering in the summer, there was always something to be done, and we did it as a family every Sunday morning before I had gone to the war. It was hard work and I liked it much less the older I got. Yet, it instilled in me the knowledge that no feeling is quite so comfortably satisfying as enjoying the aesthetic fruits of dirty, hard labor.

My mother was determined with everything in her to spend a day together. A whole day, like we used to when I was young. I cannot say that my father was in exactly good spirits, but he was receptive enough to the day that by the time I got up around nine o'clock, he had already started frying bacon for breakfast. He rarely cooked, but when he did, it was always Sunday breakfast, and they were some of the best meals I'd ever eaten. He started by frying a few pieces of bacon. And this was his big secret. He used the bacon grease to fry up the peppers, potatoes, and onions all together before dropping a half dozen eggs and then cheese all over the top. Then he'd make a bunch of sour dough French toast with butter and hot maple syrup. The delicious scent of frying pork fat was the first thing that hit me when I opened my bedroom door. Instead of going right to the bathroom and then back to bed, I welcomed the day with a stretch and the hopeful possibility that my postwar dreams might actually exist in the personified form of Miss Hadley Landon. Also, I felt good in hearing of an interview Robertson had for a security position at a local Bank. My dad always said it was important for a man to work, not for other people, but to keep his own mind right. Robertson had texted me about it early that morning. I was glad he was up early.

[Robertson]
Just got done with the interview. Nailed it.

[Me]
Right on man. What's the job for again?

[Robertson]

Security job

[Me]
Right on man. You're obviously a fucking shoe-in.

[Robertson]
Goddamn right. Bank will be a fucking fortress while I'm there.

[Me]
Hey congrats man. I know you'll get it.

And I knew he needed it. A man should be able to catch a few breaks after doing what Robertson had done.

It was a bright and warm morning. The clouds that held the heat in had parted in time to welcome the new morning sun. The birds were many and their songs were louder and it seemed like it all meant something good. My father was still in his boxing shorts and white t-shirt. It made me feel good knowing that he still hadn't altered his morning cooking attire since I'd left. He must have heard my footsteps coming into the kitchen because aside from his cooking, there was no other noise in the house. He didn't turn around, he just kept facing the stove.

As soon as I walked in he said, "You want some coffee? There's some hot up here if you want some."

He drank a whole pot himself every morning.

"I'm good for now. I think I might get some orange juice maybe," I said.

"Still don't drink coffee, huh?"

"I did when I was still in. But I had to get up at five in the morning, so that's the big reason why. I guess, no, I haven't really been drinking coffee at all since I got out. Haven't had any trouble staying awake since I got back." I couldn't tell if he acknowledged with a slight nod of his head or not. Probably not.

"Well there's some up here for you if you change your mind." He said without facing me.

The sound of crackling bacon was all that I could hear over the small chirping birds that I watched through our floor to ceiling kitchen windows, and heard through the open screen door that led to our balcony that overlooked the gazebo that my mother occupied most of her post retirement time perfecting. My dad never watched the news or listened to music in the mornings. He got his news from the newspaper and he only listened to music while he was driving and during Christmas. I liked that there was nothing but the sounds of the morning; it had been years since I had stopped to listen to them.

My father never made himself really open for conversation, and even less so in the morning. There was so much that I wanted to say to him, and to ask him, and for him to ask me, but I knew that it wasn't his way. After a few minutes sitting at our kitchen table in silence while he cooked, I realized without a doubt that he wasn't going to turn from what he was doing until he was completely done. I liked watching my father cook though. It made me feel like a boy again. There was something nice about being in somebody else's care.

I broke the comfortable silence with an awkward, "How was fishing yesterday?"

And that did it, he turned around halfway so he was partly facing me and partly facing the stove and said, "It was pretty slow. Only got a few bites and nothing worth keeping. Bill asked about you though."

"Wild Bill?" I asked."

My father laughed a little and said, "Yeah, Wild Bill."

My father had only two friends that I had ever heard of. One was killed in Vietnam and the other wasn't, and that was Bill, 'Wild Bill', as my uncle and father called him when I was a kid.

"Yeah, I told him that you'd been back for a couple of months now and he told me to tell you to give him a call. But you know, it was Bill, so he didn't exactly say it like that."

"I will, yeah. Have you not seen him in a while or something?"

"Well, he's been having a few problems. Doctors appointments and things."

"Is he all right?"

"Well, he's got the same thing your grandpa had."

"Cancer?"

"Prostate it looks like."

"Is he going to be okay?"

"Well, that's not even what got your grandpa, so who knows. Remember, the doctors said he could have lived another twenty years with it, that it wasn't even worth bothering with at his age."

It was quite a panic when my grandfather was diagnosed, but like the doctor said, he died of heart failure long before the cancer set in.

"So, he'll be okay you think?"

"From the way he talks, I'm sure everything will be fine."

"Well, that's good. That sucks though still. Is he going to have to have surgery?"

"Don't know yet."

"Goddamn, I can't believe it. I mean Bill. Who'd have thought?"

"It's just a part of getting old."

Aside from a hamstring injury ending his college track career, my father had never had an unhealthy day in his life. He turned back around toward the stove and I knew the conversation was over.

I went over to the kitchen door that led to the balcony outside. I walked out and saw my mother below. She looked up as soon as I came out. She knew I was there even though my bare feet could not have made a noticeable noise on the balcony above her.

She put her hand over her brow to block the already shining sun, looked up at me and said in a loud and happy voice, "You should come down here and join me. It'd be good for you."

I smiled at her and waved my hand like it was too early for work.

She said, "Go put some shoes on and come down here a minute."

My dad shouted from inside, "Go on down there. It'll be another twenty minutes at least before this is done. Grab a piece of bacon on your way down though. I'm cooking more, those were just for the grease."

The bacon was tender and the fat was seasoned with pepper and my taste buds told me it was going to be a good day. Things shined a little brighter on this morning and everything gave me that pleasant tingling feeling of excited anticipation right under my skin. Some days just feel right like that, like things are okay in the universe. I didn't remember feeling like that in years.

My mother was wearing short but very baggy shorts that her petite body almost got lost in. Her faded black t-shirt was one that I used to wear, and still faintly displayed the local sports team logo that was on the front. She was meticulously watering her various plants in the left-middle portion of her main flowerbed.

"You're up early," she said.

"It's past nine."

"You've been sleeping 'til almost eleven some mornings."

"I went to bed early last night."

"You and Kevin went downtown again, right?"

"Yeah."

"Have you guys had any luck finding an apartment? From what I remember, it was tough to find something affordable even in my day. I can't even imagine how it is now."

"We've seen a few places that might work all right."

"Kevin probably doesn't know downtown too much more than you do since he lived in Corvallis?"

"He came up all the time during breaks and stuff, but no, he doesn't really know downtown that well. But it's all good. Roger is going to show us around a bunch when he gets back."

"And how *is* Roger?"

"He's good. He's been in South America for the past few months, I guess."

"That sounds like Roger. So, what did you and Kevin end up doing yesterday?"

"We went to this artsy place in South Portland. It's called Strega."

"I've never heard of it, but that doesn't mean anything, I don't think I've been to any kind of bar for about thirty-five years. You had fun though?"

"Yeah, I didn't really drink much or anything." That was an obvious lie and my mother knew it but didn't show it. "They were doing poetry readings. I guess they do them every Saturday. They were kinda cool though, actually." I continued.

"Well I'm really glad you went to that. Your dad and I used to do stuff like that when we were your age, about a hundred and fifty years ago."

"Yeah? I can't see dad going to something like that."

"Oh yeah, your dad was young once too. And very social. He really liked stuff like that, even more than I did at that time. Yeah, we went to poetry readings and art galleries and your dad would get in these long political and philosophical discussions with whoever wanted to join in. Things were a lot different back then, of course. Your dad could talk, let me tell you, I think it's one of the reasons I liked him so much at first." She looked away from me with a smile and gazed into her flowers beds. Breathing slowly and deeply and then out again. She added, "A man shouldn't be afraid to say what he believes."

CHAPTER FOURTEEN
Introducing Paul McPherson

A WEEK HAD GONE by since I had last seen Hadley and everyday felt longer than the last. With exception to a day hike Kevin and I went on earlier in the week, I hadn't left the house since seeing her the past Saturday. A cousin of mine, who was two years older than me, came over to the house with her husband and newborn child to see me. We hadn't seen each other since before I'd left for the army and the real reason she came was to show off her new family. I liked seeing her but her husband seemed like a scared boy and I wondered how he ever made her happy. But she seemed happy enough, and in a real way. Her baby was a boy and called Jackson, which I thought was a stupid name but tried to act like I thought it was unique and a good name. I felt no special affection toward the child, despite it being kin to me. It cried mostly. My mother was enthralled and my father was at least as disinterested in the whole thing as I was.

Robertson called the next day and we spoke for a short time. It was starting to be a call and response kind of thing we had going together. Like a couple of old blues players going back and forth with their stories. No guitars though, just words.

"Hello."

"Hey buddy."

"Hey what's up, man?"

"Just chillin', man. How 'bout you?"

His words were slow and hung on his lips until they fell out in a jumbled sentence with no spacing between words. You would have thought that I called him.

"Same man. Just hanging out at home. What you been up to?" I said.

"Not a goddamn thing. Seeing what you're up to," he said.

"Not much man. Had lunch with my mom earlier. Saw some dude panhandling downtown with a Second Infantry patch. Vietnam," I said.

"Fuck, if something doesn't break on my end soon that's gonna be me," he said.

"What'd you mean man? That bank hit you back up yet?" I asked, with an emphasized concern that I immediately regretted expressing

"Haven't heard shit," he said.

"What the fuck, dude; who the fuck else would they have hired?" I said.

"Prolly some police academy reject or ROTC drop out."

There was no humor to his tone. Only scorn. And his words were getting sharper.

"They just gotta go through all the applicants I'm sure. There's no way you aren't getting hired, man," I said and hoped my words were at least a little convincing.

"Yeah, hopefully. I can't just keep living off my mom. And the fucking VA. They aren't doing shit for me, man. After all that shit with my dad, and then I do two fucking tours, I'll tell you, buddy, they don't give a shit about you once you take off that uniform. Don't matter what you did," he said.

"Don't worry about it too much, man. You're gonna get that bank gig and everything's gonna be fine in a few weeks man. You'll see," I said.

"Yeah, I'll see. Until I don't," he said.

"Na man. It's gonna be fine, man. Trust me, dude. You're Specialist Chris Fucking Robertson, two time vet of the harshest theaters of combat in two countries. Unless they got Audie Murphy him-fucking-self preserved in the back somewhere, you're the best man for the job," I said.,

"Fucking, Drew. It's fucking good talking to you again, man. I fucking missed you this last year, buddy. Never thought things would be like this."

For the first time in the conversation, his voice had some life in it.

"Yeah, we're still here though, man. Remember, there was a time when neither of us knew if we'd see 21," I said.

"Amen, buddy." There was a long pause and I liked to have thought we both felt a little better than before. "Well listen, I'll let you get back, but hit me up soon, buddy," he added.

"Will do. Peace, man," I said.

It was different talking to Robertson than it was my other friends. Of course it was. Robertson didn't have any other friends. I should have called him before I did. It was starting to become a little clearer how he felt. As the days went and things didn't get easier, it got a lot worse. All that anxious tension we carried back with us. It all made sense; we killed people and people tried to kill us. It was high stress work, but you think as you come home and live a normal life that things will go back to normal. But they don't. You're that same person, the killer, what are we even supposed to do?

Kevin didn't want to go with me to Strega that week. I think he was sore that the last week didn't pan out. I didn't care. There was really no one else to ask and I wouldn't have wanted anybody else there anyway.

The bar was more crowded than it had been before. It was also warmer than it had been. Instead of ordering a drink, I waited outside and smoked a couple of cigarettes. I liked being there be-cause my thoughts were different. I thought about Hadley and my conversation from the week before. She spoke of Virginia Woolf as one of her favorite writers. I found a book by Virginia Woolf, *Mrs. Dalloway*, in my mother's collection. I read it in two days. Her characters were very real, even more than Hemingway's who writes with too much pride to be as real as Woolf. I think that's the same way Hadley wrote her poetry; completely exposed. I wish Robertson had a Hadley in his life. Not necessarily to have, because I didn't even have her, but just to know she was there; that things like her were real.

Waiting for the performances to begin with my cold beer, I stood just outside the door and smoked another cigarette. Not knowing which way Hadley would come, I stood keeping an open view of both entrance points. I wanted to be the first person there to see her. I wanted to be the first person to see her always - every day. Daydreams from the week before had recreated the entire picturesque scene. Accuracy, however sparse, it was Hadley just the same. I had her locked in my mind's eye forever and rejoiced at the idea of keeping her there for only me to see. She looked so beautiful onstage. I don't believe in angels or any of that fluff, but she wasn't human, couldn't be. Nothing that perfect.

It wouldn't have mattered what she wore, what her hair looked like or whether she didn't have any makeup on or anything. Hadley couldn't be plain if she tried. An eminent glow radiated from every pore of her body and there isn't a thing she could do to hold it back. She was infinitely and absolutely perfectly beautiful. I thought she was sexy as hell too. There's a real difference between a woman being beautiful and being sexy. A lot of girls can be one or the other, but it's really hard to be both. It's strange, but it seems like being one so often makes you less the other. Hadley was both.

I couldn't remember her poem perfectly, but thought about it in a more abstract manner. Sometimes you don't have to remember something to remember how it made you feel. That's how Hadley's poem was for me.

Before Hadley, an old woman got on stage. She must have been close to eighty years old and reminded me of my grandmother. She had a floral pattern blouse and the same kind of tennis shoes my grandmother wore: white canvas with Velcro. She didn't much remind me of her once she started up though.

You would think an old lady like that would just talk about her grandkids and stuff if she was reading her poem, but she didn't. Her poem wasn't about that at all. It was about being born. It was a long poem, written about a doctor delivering a premature baby, but the thing about it was, that it was written from the perspective of the baby. It was like this little infant had all the wisdom of the old lady reading her poem, but didn't know what to make of any of it because she was just being brought into the world.

For some reason, it made me think of the war. I didn't want to, not in the middle of all that. There's nothing worse than watching a good movie or hearing a good poem and having it remind you of things that you don't want to think about. My armpits got all sweaty like they usually did whenever I thought about the war. I had to go into the bathroom and wipe off some of the sweat with a brown paper towel. My stomach started to knot up and I felt tremendous pressure in the front of my head. I splashed cold water against my face and cupped handfuls into my dry cottony mouth. This was the reason I didn't leave the house. Because it happened almost every time. I didn't know why, I couldn't see it coming and certainly couldn't stop it once it did. I had to just wait it out, by myself, in the bathroom, hoping nobody took too close a notice.

Finally, I left the bathroom, ordered my third beer, and went out and smoked another cigarette. There were too many people there; I don't know that there were any more than any other week, but they seemed to be really squeezing in on me.

Everything stopped when Hadley came in. At least it did for me. The rest of the world kept on going, I just didn't care what it did anymore. I was a bit of a wreck, still sweaty, hands clammy, I didn't care once I saw her. She came to me as soon as she walked in. She looked like a movie star. Hadley walked with a lot of movement in her shoulders and neck. Her hair was the color of uncut wheat and the light shown threw it, making it glow around her. I imagined her not as a person. but a magical pixie floating in my own personal dream world.

With my best James Dean pose, I leaned against the inside of the open front door and looked up at her from tilted eyes. Fighting back my smile that wanted to open a mile wide, I pushed myself upright as she approached. Her own smile widened with each nearing step. Her arms raised in the air and I mirrored her motion. My heart felt as though it were going to pound out of my chest. We had never touched before. Maybe we shook hands the first time we met, but now a hug? I questioned nothing and couldn't wait for her warm body and taut breasts to press against my own quivering body. My arms went up and I felt somebody bump against my back shoulder. As she came toward me, I saw that her eyes were not on me, but looking just past me. A tall young man wearing a fitted T-shirt that read, Oregon Highway Patrol, casually displaced me with his broad shoulders and took Hadley into his arms.

Rushes of hot blood went to all the bad parts of my body and my armpits were instant swamps of perspiration. That same kind of nausea came back to me and I went back out the door and hoped like hell that she hadn't seen me. I screamed a thousand silent screams of anger and rejection and hatred and lit another cigarette.

A boyfriend. And what a boyfriend. I knew, because I knew *him*. He was three years ahead of me in school and I still remembered him well, even though he didn't remember me at all. Paul McPherson was tall, handsome, strong, and dressed really nicely. But that's not even what impressed people about him. Paul could talk. He could talk to anybody about damn near anything, and he did. He really was a smart and friendly guy. He was a cop too, which I didn't like much because I thought he should be dumb and aggressive like I thought most cops were. The only thing that gave him away was the T-shirt. I hated him so much. He was one of those guys who just seemed to do everything so goddamn effortlessly. That's how he was in high school, and that's still how he was when I saw him with Hadley.

I went back inside for no other reason than to pay my bar tab. Hadley was sitting at a table in the far corner next to the front door with Paul. I hoped she wouldn't see me and I tried my best to shelter myself behind the line of people while I paid for my drinks. I don't know who scared who more when Hadley surprised me with her hand around my arm and I swung around as I was signing my tab.

"Drew. I didn't see you here before. Are you leaving?"

"No, no. I'm not leaving. I just wanted to pay my tab now with my card, switching to cash after this," I said nonsensically.

"Oh. Oh okay. Well, when you're done, you want to come over here and sit with us? We should have a drink together."

She was motioning over toward her table with Paul. He was looking at the painting on the wall and didn't see either of us. Hesitant as I was, there was nothing else to do. I sat down with them and we all shared a round. When Hadley introduced us, I pretended not to know who he was, knowing he didn't remember me. We all talked and Paul was very polite to me but not even in that phony way that most really good-looking people are polite to you; he really was just a nice polite guy and it made sense that Hadley would adore him as much as I hated him. She was happy to see me but that didn't matter much at that point. I asked her if she was going to read anything and she said that she was. Just as she was about to say something else, Paul leaned over her shoulder and kissed her hard on the lips, then kissed her once on the forehead, and looked at her the way I wanted to be able to look at her. She was happy, but subdued. Her smile was comfortable and natural but it was smaller than I had seen it when she was without Paul, and she didn't radiate the same kind of energetic glow with him there. I knew that I could make her glow and it bothered me that Paul wasn't able to let her shine as brightly as she should have. She giggled as she pulled away from his arms, and laughed out loud as he pulled her back in for a passionate kiss before she got up on stage.

As soon as she got on stage and started reciting, Paul went to the bar to get a drink and then went outside. I left in the middle of Hadley's poem because I couldn't stand to be in that bar for another more minute. I said goodbye to Paul as I passed him in the back parking lot. talking on his cell phone. He said nothing to me and just smiled silently like we were old friends. I drove away gripping the steering wheel so hard that by the time I got home, my hands were burning with stinging exhaustion and white-knuckle tension. I went up to my bedroom without saying anything to my parents who were downstairs watching a movie like they did almost every night. I got the half empty vodka bottle from the bottom of my army duffel bag where I buried it and got drunk in my room.

Robertson called later that evening. I was not awake and it took me a few minutes to become alert. I don't remember what he talked about at first. I hadn't told him about Hadley or anything I was doing really so I never brought up Paul. We talked about dreams. We were both very drunk.

I said something like, "Recurring dreams are cool. I used to have the same dream over and over when I was a kid. I was playing baseball in a brightly colored animated stadium, and I was normal, but the stadium and the other players were all cartoons, and they weren't real players at all. They were all like circus animals or something. I remember an elephant; he had long eyelashes and wore a small flower-patterned hat. And he would hit homeruns every time at bat," I said.

"Sounds like it was a girl to me," he said.

"Who?"

"The elephant," he said.

"Oh, shit. Yeah, maybe. Never thought about that. I don't think they could talk," I said.

Robertson cleared his throat and said, "When I was a little kid I used to have this dream like I was out in a giant open meadow that didn't seem to have any end to it at all. Like in the dream the whole world could have been just this big bright open meadow with shin high grass and a warm sun and just the right amount of clouds. The wind would always be blowing at just the right speed to feel good on my skin and it would move the grass together like it was moving to music. That's when I would get all tight and I'd want to just escape inside myself. When I felt that wind I knew it was over. That's how it came at me every time. I'd feel the wind and then I'd look up at the sun. It'd be covered by a cloud and then it would get cold and dark and thunder would come from out of nowhere and then suddenly everything would go black. I'd look back down from the sky and turn back from where I'd just been and there'd be nothing there but a rocky cliff, my heels just inches from the edge. Nothing on the other side. I'd look back up at the sky, I don't know at God or something, I guess, and that would be all I could ever remember," he said.

"Jesus, man. You had that more than once?" I asked.

"Couple times a week at least. Still do sometimes, but now it's different. Now I don't look up afterward anymore, I just keep walking forward," he said.

"The only shitty one I ever had was that I was running from somebody. I don't know if it was always the same person or who it was; I don't think it mattered. I could never see them anyway. I just somehow knew that they were there. And it always felt like they were going to catch me. And then sometimes, when I'd try to run as fast as I could, my legs just wouldn't work. It would feel like I was wading through a waist deep pool of Georgia mud; I just couldn't go anywhere. Finally, I'd exhaust myself almost to the point of passing out, I'd turn around to whatever was chasing me, like I was going to fight it out with them or something. But then when they got close, I couldn't ever hit them. I just kept missing and when I'd finally get them, my punches did nothing and I could tell I was going to lose. I never did though. The fights always just ended somehow. I never even saw who it was coming after me. I just knew they were there, and then all of a sudden they wouldn't be, and that'd be all I could remember," I said.

"Maybe it was you. The person you were running from. Maybe that's why you could never see them, even when you knew they were close," he said in an assured tone.

"Fuck, man, I don't know; that was a long time ago. I haven't had one of those for years now. I can't remember the last dream I had," I said not wanting to think any more of it.

"All I usually do in mine now is sit in a room alone. It's usually the same goddamn room too."

"In your dream?" I asked.

"Yeah, I have it all the time lately. It's hot, but dry like Iraq and I'm at a chair and a small wooden desk. Some light is coming from the door but I never look at it in the dream or anything. There's always a piece of paper I'm staring at. A note or something on the desk. I'm just sitting there by myself holding a pen in my hand and staring down at this paper, but nothing's written on it yet. I don't know. I've been having it every night now for the last couple weeks," he said.

"That's kinda creepy, yeah. I think you're watching too many horror movies late at night or something, man."

"Yeah, can't really sleep too well," he said.

"I know. Me either man. You should try smoking. I smoked some with a friend the other night and it was the best sleep I'd gotten in years," I said.

"Na. Never been my thing," he said.

"Guess it's not as common a thing out there," I said.

"Yeah you guys have it with your cereal in the morning," he said with a forced single chuckle.

"Better than coffee," I said.

"Ah, I miss you, Hoskins. I'll let you get back though, buddy; it was nice talking to you," he said.

Back to what, I don't know. It was the middle of the night, two hours later for him, and we were both drunk.

"Take it easy man," I said. I could have talked for another hour and would rather have. It was nice to talk to somebody about something other than where to go that night for drinks. It didn't take long though for thoughts of Hadley to drift back into my mind. I thought about her and I thought about Paul and how they were probably together in bed somewhere sleeping next to each other, her arm around his chest, delicate breaths on his neck. I finished my bottle and went to the dark kitchen and ate a banana and went to sleep on the living room couch.

CHAPTER FIFTEEN
Who Says Chivalry Is Dead?

KEVIN AND THE REST of the guys were out, as usual, for a Saturday and they had met up with some girls they knew from the university. He called me a few times trying to get me to meet up with them at a bar in midtown. I didn't care about the girls and I knew they'd only make me miss Hadley.

An urging tone from my mother who had overheard the phone call got me to go more than anything. My isolation had become routine and I hadn't left the house since learning of Paul. My mother was quietly concerned about my disinterest in all things peripheral to my childhood home. I began to sense in her a sadness that I hadn't seen since my first deployment, as if she knew that whatever it was I had seen and done had gotten to a place that she could never heal.

The war had come biting back harder than it had the weeks before when I still had Hadley to keep me occupied. The more I thought about combat, the harder it was to think about anything else. It's not how you might think though. I don't know exactly what people think combat vets think about when they think about war, but I'm sure it's something very different from what it was for me. It wasn't about the killing, not much anyway. Killing people is what I think of the least often. It's different than that. It's more of a feeling than a thought process. A state of being more than a conscious action. Sensations are heightened. I feel it in my body first. The images and memories come after and are all distorted. I don't know how real they are anymore.

It's like when you were a kid, at least with me anyway. I don't really have specific memories of being a little kid. It's more like I remember recollections. It's really spaced out, like an amnesiac watching home movies of his family and having an uncanny feeling of peculiar familiarity. I know it was me who was there and did and saw the things I did, I just can't quite place myself at the scene. Sometimes I feel like I actually died in the streets that night in Iraq and I'm just a ghost of myself living in some strange purgatorial existence, devoid of all reason.

I think Dante wrote something about that but I don't remember that either. At least I had Robertson to talk to. I wish I could have been a little bit better for him though. I wish I could have had something better to say most of the time. I hoped that in hearing of my problems he would be more comfortable with his own and not just burdened by mine. Regrettably, it's all I had to give him.

[Me]
You still think about things man?

[Robertson]
Every day since I left.

[Me]
Me too. I was just wondering because I just got out.

[Robertson]
Over a year now for me. Don't think it'll ever change. Still wake up twice a night looking for my rifle.

[Me]
Fuck man. That sucks. I didn't think it'd be like this. I don't know how I thought it was going to be.

[Robertson]
Me either.

[Me]
You still talk to Blemly or Adkins or anybody?

[Robertson]
Not really.

[Me]
Wonder what they're up to.

[Robertson]
Nothing. Nobody's done shit.

[Me]
Whatever. You're doing fine man.

[Robertson]
Am I?

[Me]
You made it out man. Did the bank give you a call back yet or what?

[Robertson]
No.

[Me]
Well they probably got a lot of applicants to go through and stuff. They have to go through all them by procedure anyway, even if they know who they're going to hire. I'm sure you'll get it man.

[Robertson]
Yeah

[Me]
You doing alright man?

[Robertson]
Fine

[Me]
You should come out here man.

[Robertson]
Where

[Me]
To my house here in Oregon. We can go in the city and drink and stuff, I got a cool bar I go to. You'd like it. You always said you wanted to come out west.

[Robertson]
Cant

[Me]
Just for a few days man.

[Robertson]
No money cant

[Me]
You'd stay with me man. We'd just eat food at my house and my parents would take us out to dinner like every night too. It'd just be the plane ticket.

[Robertson]
Still too much

[Me]
I could buy your plane ticket man. I still got plenty of money left. Call it a late birthday present, man.

[Robertson]
No

[Me]
I'm buying it for you. It's as much a present to me as it is to you. I want to see you again.

My phone seemed to ring as the message was still sending. It was Robertson. There was no greeting. As I answered, the first vowel sounds were already coming through the receiver, "I don't want to come there. I have stuff to do here. I can't just pick up and leave for Oregon. I need to find a job, *okay*."

"Yeah I just thought that—"

"I know, but you gotta fucking realize that I have things going on here too, I can't just leave whenever. Who'd help my mom take care of things when I was gone? I mean who'd stay here with her. I can't just leave. Thanks, I get it and everything, but no."

"Just think about it a bit man."

"*No!*"

"Fine man. Whatever."

"You know what? *Fuck you Hoskins.* You don't know shit alright? With your fucking bullshit life there in *fucking Oregon* with your *fucking bitches* and friends and *fucking bars* and shit to go to. *What the fuck do you know about it how it is here?* You came home to a fucking paradise. I came home to a fucking shit hole. I'd rather still be in. At least I fucking meant something. Nobody gives a fuck now. *Nobody!*"

I was sickened. I'd made it worse. I thought Robertson was a way for me to hold on to something that I couldn't shake away anyway, but that's not at all what it was. Robertson was a way for me to feel better about myself. He was somebody who was and would always do worse and there was an assured consistency in this fact that had brought a subconscious ease to my own selfish pangs that I did not realize until he said what he did. I didn't get it. His plight was more foreign to me than mine was to Kevin. While Robertson and I shared in an experience more peculiar and intimate than any other I know, we had come from, and since returned, to different worlds.

When I met up with Kevin and the rest of them, they were all drunk and concerned with their own affairs. It was better being with them because I didn't have to think about Robertson, or Paul, or me. My friend Jason, who was also there during the wine walk when I got kicked out of the bar, had a rather ugly girl with him. He was shooting whiskey, which was always the fastest remedy for the less than desirable aesthetic appeal of a boring and thoughtless girl. He was smashed and I had no problem partaking in the somewhat ritualistic game of dueling shot glasses. The game was nothing if not simple. It consisted of two participants, two glasses, and a bottle of hard liquor. The first participant would have a shot and the other would follow and this would continue until one of the participants couldn't go on. The bartender was accommodating. Some drink pourers reserve a semblance of responsibility in rationing out the last legal drug to a thirsty patron, but lucky for us, he held no such reservations. And I wanted drink. After a few shots, the conversation with Robertson became inescapable from my consciousness. Sometimes whiskey would clean out the cobwebs and sometimes it would just sink you deeper and deeper with every drop. The liquor washed away all emotion but guilt. Selfish fucking guilt. I drank more and my demeanor became reminiscent of my infantry days and I was probably looking for a fight from the very beginning.

It was actually Kevin who noticed first, but I was the one who said something. What began as a mere distraction and made its way quickly to a mild annoyance, had become too caustic a scene for me not to involve myself. It was a bar very different from Strega. It was a dive all the same but the atmosphere, and more significantly, the patrons, were not of the same variety that I had grown accustomed to. This place had a pool table and covered sports on all the TVs. Strega had a stage for performances and not a single TV in the bar. This wasn't my scene but the whiskey placed me there comfortably enough before I meddled in what we all shamefully watched from afar. Chivalry was not a factor but I suppose at the time it's the bullshit notion I would have claimed preservation of.

I approached the four of them as they played on the only pool table in the bar. Two women and two men, each about the same age, maybe a couple of years older than Jason, Kevin, and myself. The smaller couple exchanged the harshest words. The slightly more reserved couple were both very fat and the man had a shaved bald head and very large and unkempt mutton-chop sideburns. He had on a leather vest with a large patch on the back that didn't belong to any of the three notorious motorcycle gangs in the region. The woman's hair was dirty blonde and sat in greasy curls just past her obtuse jaw line and blunted chin. They both chuckled at the smaller man's words toward the smaller woman as their neck fat jiggled with their laughs. They looked like a couple of white trash water beds after a kid just jumped up and down on them. I was less than amused as I heard their primitive diatribe and observed their borderline abusive behavior toward their somehow compliant women. I had come from the infantry. My friends, save for Kevin, were not quire boys, but these guys were just shit.

The whiskey burned on my tongue from the last shot and the fermented sting and my misguided drunken fervor coalesced. Had his violations only gone so far as to continually address his female companion with the endearing title of 'bitch', I may not have said anything. I have no special distaste for men who treat their women badly but when that barbaric treatment extends to a physical gesture, however trivial that gesture may be, I am compelled, as I suspect all men are, to interfere in the association. He was handling her arm in a way that was too aggressive by my judgment. I can't say how I would have seen it through sober eyes. Perhaps I should have better chosen my battle.

"Hey man, why don't you watch what the fuck you say to your lady." My words were not chosen carefully. I was caustic from the outset, seeking conflict from first word.

The much larger of the two put his hand out in front of the small one I was addressing and looked at me with scorn and said, "Excuse me? You talking to us or something?"

I felt all eyes on the bar go to my back, but knew that's all that was there. I couldn't see any of my friends from my peripherals but didn't care and knew I was too far in to hesitate. The two women stood by their men with a level of allegiance in their eyes I had not seen since the battlefield.

"Yeah, I'm talking to your friend here, man. Everybody can hear you guys. Nobody wants to see that shit, man. I mean come on, we're all just trying to have a good time. Why don't you just chill out on all that while you're here? Take it easy on the girl for Christ's sake." I answered.

The four of them shared a small laugh until the smaller of the men squeezed his hand around his girl's shoulder, silencing her immediately.

"Why don't you take your little ass back to your table with the rest of your *faggot* friends and let us play our game?"

The big one who said it looked serious, but the smaller one was smiling at me again.

"Look dude, I don't give a shit what you say to me or anybody else. Just chill out on all that shit with your girl, okay?"

I hoped that would end it but I was sure that it wouldn't. The small one took a step back as the big one took one forward, putting himself eyeball to eyeball with me. His breath was that of an old dog. He had spit all over his lips and his eyes were bloodshot and peering down at me and it was at this point that I took notice of his great size.

He put his finger to my chest and yelled into my already burning hot face, "Well guess what mother fucker; *this little bitch over here* is his *wife* and *my sister*, and I say he can talk to her however the fuck he wants!"

It was a point-of-no-return kind of situation. I did not hesitate to raise first arms. Making sure to reserve enough for accuracy, I put everything I had behind my fist which landed not at all to either side of his wet mouth, but right in the center, so as to smash his lips right up against his dirty teeth and send his head flying back like he'd just been rear-ended by a school bus. Just as the glorious strike registered, I received one of my own to the right side of my face. The weasely little fucker had flanked me in the middle of all that fury and landed what I still recall as the most debilitating punch I have ever endured.

I wasn't rightly knocked out, but close. Stunned as I was, the first punch did not send me to the ground, but he wisely threw another in its direct aftermath, and this one certainly did. By this time, at least Kevin had come to my rescue enough to ensure the big one wasn't going to do me any damage. Kevin took a pool cue to the big guy's head. The small one fled as I came to my feet.

I saw Kevin standing above the big one with the cue reared back like a baseball bat and looked down at the fat trash and screamed into his bleeding face, *"Get up and I'll put this right across your fucking head!"*

Jason was still on the other side of the bar, his arms clenched around his ugly companion as if they just witnessed some kind of horrible massacre.

My face didn't hurt at all, but I was dizzy from both the adrenaline and the punches to the head. I looked down at the fat leathered man but had nothing to say. Looking down at him injured and hurting the way he was, I thought of a time in Afghanistan when I came upon a wounded enemy fighter and shot him between the eyes as he reached out for me. He wore the same look as they all did and I was bothered in seeing it. The bartender, who had watched the whole thing transpire with the rest of his patrons, gave us a quick sympathetic warning that the police were on their way. I offered to pay our tab, but he said there was no need to and that we were welcome back anytime, but that we should leave right away.

There was something peculiarly unsatisfying in the direct aftermath of that fight. Kevin and I went to another bar. My face was not bloodied and only swollen and not yet bruised. I decided I wanted another drink and Kevin, shaken as he was, never having been in a real fight before then, was open to the idea of another drink before calling it a night. We went over the contents of the entire event for well over an hour, the story changing each time it was recreated. We got drunker and I was a little sad for some reason. As I said, for whatever reason, this fight did not carry with it the splendor that the others before it always had. I grew tired of the conversation but could tell that Kevin wanted to keep talking about it.

I saw a side of him that I never had before. He'd never seen it either. He liked it much better than I did. I told Kevin that I was tired and was going to go home. He told me to stay and that I wasn't able to drive and I told him what he could do with that and left him there by himself, his hands were still trembling with adrenaline as I left.

It was just past midnight when I arrived home and the drive only gave the alcohol more time to take its affect. I was already very drunk before going to the last bar, and possibly concussed from the beating I just took, but was happy that I didn't kill myself or any pedestrians on the drive home.

My mother did not share in my optimism. I had considerable trouble with my keys and my right arm unknowingly leaned against the doorbell while fumbling with the metallic instruments.

"Drew, what are you doing? Why do you keep ringing the bell?" She said as she opened the door in her blue night robe and slippers.

"It's just, it's it for me mom, I had to come home. I don't want to go out there anymore, Mom."

My words were very slow to come out and ran together when they did, but she understood me all the same.

"Did you drive? I told you to call me if you needed to."

I came into the light of the entrance hall and upon noticing my punch-swollen face, she turned more motherly than disciplinary and put her hands on my cheeks. Her eyes filled with tears and she put her arms around me and I began to cry. She asked me what had happened but I didn't say anything. I didn't want to lie to her but I couldn't tell her the truth even though I didn't think it was anything that bad.

Sometimes it's hard to tell your mom the truth, even when it's not that bad. My father stayed in bed and my mother took me into the kitchen and fixed me an ice pack and gave me some water. I sat at our round wooden dinner table, the same one I grew up eating around and held a special affinity for still. She wanted to know what had happened but didn't ask me again. She asked me if I wanted to be alone but I liked her being there and we talked about my grand-mother, among other subjects, for the next hour. Hesitant as she was, I insisted that I was okay and implored her to go to bed, assuring her that I'd be fine in the morning.

After she went to bed, I turned off the light in the kitchen and sat silently in the dark and drank another glass of water. I emptied my pockets on the kitchen table where I sat: cell phone, wallet, keys, knife.

My grandpa told me once as a kid, "I never met a man worth his weight in shit who didn't carry a knife on him."

I was about eight, I think, when he said it and have carried one on me since. This is the one I'd carried in my pocket through three tours of combat. Half serrated four-inch blade, black plastic grip, thumb-release lock back. I opened it slowly. Holding it in my right hand I pressed my left index finger down hard on the tip. I dragged my finger down the blade gently and remembered hearing in a movie that if you were going to slit your wrist you had to do it the long way, parallel with your arm, and not straight across like they usu-ally show people do. I ran the blade up and down my arm, pressing gently at first and then slightly harder, then harder still, making a small cut that I was too drunk to feel on the last swipe. There was some blood that I soaked up with a paper towel but it stopped almost immediately and I watched as the blood soaked into the porous paper.

I opened the door out to our balcony and felt the still warm night air on my swollen face. Deep breaths through my nose escaped in long sighs threw my mouth and I left it open and tasted the northwest dew. I was out of cigarettes so I went back inside and got one from the pack my mother always kept right next to the kitchen sink. Her cigarettes were feminine, marketed toward woman, meaning only that they had a light blue and bright pink pattern on the front of the pack. They tasted different but good and I thought about smoking another brand myself. I folded the knife back up after smoking the cigarette, walked back inside and set it down diagonally across my brown leather wallet.

Once inside, I poured myself another glass of water and walked to the fridge where my mother had a heart shaped magnet with a mirror built into it. It was still unsettling to look at my reflection but I remember thinking about it right then and wondering what it was I was trying to see in it but no longer could. Without turning on any lights, I walked into the living room, which was connected to our kitchen by an open doorway. The room was very grandiose, the kind of room I imagined rich people dined in. What had escaped my understanding as a child for no other reason than that I was simply accustomed to the association, I suddenly, and for the first time understood, that however horrific my experiences of the last few years had been, I had come from a place of greater advantage than probably anybody I had known.

I felt like a stranger in my own home and wondered when exactly I had forgotten what life was like before the war. Instead of turning on any lights, I pulled my lighter from my pocket and used it as a guiding torch as though I were some nineteenth century excavator looking for relics of a lost civilization. The burning flame led me to the picture that looked more real than it ever had before.

There it was, that same picture. The moon landing. It hung there triumphantly and seemingly unmoved since the day I remembered first taking its notice as a child. It must have been something about the flames flickering light that drew me in like never before. My thumb burned and I let the flame disappear. I stood in the dark, the thick moonlight shined through the white gossamer drape linings and gave the image a new perspective that I couldn't help but examine. I pulled a chair from the table and crossed my right leg over my left and lit the flame in front of the picture.

Leaning in, I saw something in it that I had never looked at in such a way. It was an eye. Large but somehow distant and faded within the picture like a watermark. What I was seeing was a reflection of my own eye. Buzz Aldrin's space helmet head eclipsed the reflection of my pupil just like the moon. I tried to hold as steady as I could, but it was only for an instant that it all lined up perfectly. My thumb got hot again and I stood up and pushed my chair back and went to bed thinking about Hadley.

CHAPTER SIXTEEN
Veterans

HER VOICE STILL SHOOK with desperate trembles. She cried when she heard my voice. It wasn't a reminder. She hadn't stopped thinking about it for a second since she had found him. She called for a semblance of relief I guess.

The note said, "I'm very sorry, but I needed it all to just stop."

I'd never made that call before, to one of my dead soldier's mothers, telling her that her son died bravely in the midst of battle, saving the lives of his fellow paratroopers. Whatever fortune I had been granted by bypassing this conversation while still a soldier, had dissolved with what I was finding myself doing now. She called me very early in the morning from her son's phone. I saw Robertson's name on the caller ID and knew something was wrong. I didn't think it would be as bad as it was.

"Drew."

The voice was tired and broken into pieces. She wasn't crying, and she didn't ask when she said my name. She simply said it.

"Yeah, this is Drew. Is this Mrs. Robertson? Is everything alright?"

"No."

"What's the matter?" Is Robertson okay?"

"No, he isn't Drew."

Her words were clearing up but there was still a recognized terror underneath.

"What's the matter? Is he okay?"

"No, Drew. No, Drew. Chris isn't okay."

"Let me talk to him. Is he around? Just let me talk to him, Mrs. Robertson. Tell him I need to talk to him, no matter what he says."

"You ca-a-a-ant. You ca-ant talk to hi-i-i-m, Drew. You can't."

She broke apart and I hadn't heard a person cry since my mother picked me up at the airport. Her tears were very different though.

"Tell him I *have* to talk to him, Mrs. Robertson. Please trust me. I know I can talk to him."

"You can't. He's gone, Drew."

"He left his phone? Where is he?"

"They took him away, Drew. They already took him away from me, Drew."

"Who took him away Mrs. Robertson? Where did they go?" I already knew where he'd gone. I couldn't believe it though.

"He's gone Drew. He's gone. Oh, my God, Drew; my baby is gone."

"What happened Mrs. Robertson?"

"Drew, he's dead. My God, Drew, my baby is dead."

He felt something worse than me. That's why he's dead and I'm alive. His pain was greater. Robertson would be buried in Flint, Michigan next to his alcoholic father who burned villages in North Vietnam. He was like me and misinterpreted movies that depicted these atrocities. So later we would go on to commit our own.

I went to the bathroom right away. An absence of an expected nausea put anger on top of my sadness; maybe it was rage. I couldn't tell the difference anymore. Was I used to death? Was it all I knew? I looked into the mirror and wanted to rip it off the wall and shatter it into a thousand pieces and pick them up and do it over again until every piece was nothing but sand cutting into my bleeding feet. I wanted to chew off my tongue and gouge out my eyes. I remember seeing it in a movie once. There was this guy who just got back from Vietnam and he was alone in a dark and dirty hotel room sitting on the bed hunkered over a bottle of liquor, sweating, crying, and grinding his jaw. I used to watch that movie and others like it while doing pushups in front of the television, my army surplus dog tags bouncing off my mother's plush living room carpeting as I imagined it to be the dusty bare ground of infantry school. I made up, in my mind, a drill sergeant at my side personally dedicated to driving me into the ground, making me quit with all the hate and energy he could muster from his war-torn body. I could smell his tobacco in my face as I clinched my face tighter and pushed harder into the carpet until my muscles burned with the heat of a thousand chemical fires.

That I actually anticipated much of what I was now experiencing in my post war life provided no relief from my angst. On the contrary, I had another reason to hate myself. Perhaps the greatest turmoil for a sorrowed veteran comes when he finally realizes through much introspection that while he was a soldier, he attacked with steadfast and splendid vigor almost every ethical conception of the world and humanity that he now holds, in a manner so fierce and precise that it cannot be countered by anything his efforts will foster for the rest of his life. And what's more is that he must constantly and forever accept with obligatory politeness the patriotic "thank you's" for participating in those misinterpreted acts. It's a foul nature. Pure rot. And Robertson needed it to all just stop.

Something about the next few days caught the attention of my parents. I didn't say anything. There was nothing to say. Robertson was dead, and he would soon be remembered as only an early statistic. Maybe it was that I was eating less, or didn't take a shower, or maybe it was that they knew what to look for better than I did. I never told my parents about him. I didn't even talk to Kevin or Hadley about it.

My dad knew though; he knew that something was wrong. He called up his friend Bill to talk to me. I knew Wild Bill from before I could remember. I used to love the trips we would go on together, deer hunts, antelope hunts, and we used to catch some of the biggest steelhead you have ever seen. At the time, I was still just a boy and had never seen combat or even a woman naked, for that matter. Even then, before I understood it, or anything, I could tell that Bill was different from my uncle and father. He talked less and smiled smaller. He ate less on hunts and wouldn't come back to camp until well past dark. A man of few words but much compassion, I always knew he loved me. Bill was always trying to teach me things that the men in my family didn't know, like always keeping both eyes open when you shoot so as not to limit your field of visibility and to never wear deodorant on a hunt because "the deer'll smell that shit quicker than an NVA regular".

He had a powerful presence. It was like he breathed more air in than other people. Heat seemed to radiate from his body and while he stood well under six feet, his form was that of a great beast. His shoulders broad and arms always flexed with vigilance, he wore his fatigue in dusty brown eyes. His fighting days in this life were long over but in every other universe he was still burying axes into men's chests or putting rounds through their skulls. Like my grandfather, Bill's father fought in the Second Great War; a generation whose glory and national fanaticism paved the way for the enthusiastic participation in our own wars.

Bill had turned eighteen in 1969 and was never drafted. Like me, he was an eager under achieving high school kid, impatiently watching combat missions on the news while doing pushups during commercial breaks. As soon as he graduated, he went to his nearest recruitment office and five months later was patrolling Vietnamese jungles with the 101st Airborne Division. He did two tours and rarely talked about the war. We were all fishing one day years back when my uncle's friend asked him why he volunteered for a second tour of duty, and he said looking dead into his eyes, "To be judged."

Bill had contacted my father and asked to have a beer with me. I had not seen him since I was sixteen and stopped going on family hunting trips. My father had told me of his cancer and I didn't know what to expect driving to his house.

On the way, I stopped for cigarettes at a gas station. As I pulled up, I noticed a new black Cadillac in the parking lot. On the back were the same Oregon veteran license plates as I had, airborne wings and U.S Army emblem engraved respectively on each side of four random numbers. I glanced inside the car as I walked by and saw a woman inside who was well into her golden years with short silvery gray hair. Her husband must have been a WWII paratrooper and I wanted to meet and shake the man's hand. Whenever meeting an old combat vet, I'd think back to what they might have looked like when they were my age, still young and eager for battle. I walked past a few of the aisles pretending to be looking for something, but I was only looking for him. There was a middle-aged woman in the candy section and a teenager staring wonderingly at the beer, but no WWII vet that I could see. I wanted to meet the man but didn't care enough to stick around and instead went to the counter to buy cigarettes. Just as the clerk was fetching my pack, I heard the underage boy shriek out the word, *"Sick."* I looked over at him and traced his stare to the bathroom door in the far corner where an elderly man in light khaki pants and a white golf shirt shuffled his skeletal body slowly toward the door. His pants were light and you could plainly see the explosive shit that stained them like black on canvas. Everything in the store stopped and what was only a distance of twenty feet from the bathroom to the exit turned into what I'm sure felt like ten miles for that wet shit covered old paratrooper.

Whatever he had done until that moment didn't matter anymore. He was young and once strong. He loved a woman and could pick her up over his head. He fought in the Great War and fathered children and built a house. Now he was old and slow and covered in his own shit. It's funny and sad how everything in life comes full circle.

Bill didn't invite me in. I knocked and he came to the door and took me right to his truck. He was much shorter than my father and me but you couldn't really tell until you were standing next to him. He'd started going bald before I'd ever met him, but he always wore the same old blue Seattle Mariner baseball cap to cover it up. His features were blunted all around, his chin was scarcely there amongst his huge jaw bones and muscular neck. He looked as though he had always shaved three days ago and he tried to force a smile whenever somebody looked at him but it came over as more of a squeaky frown. His unseemly features and rough expression matched his experiences in war but not at all his capacity for compassion. There exists an unfortunate tendency for most people to judge books by their cover without doing so much as reading the first page. For whatever other reasons somebody could list, it was for his lack of delicacy in expression, that Bill had remained alone.

He opened the door wearing the only thing I had ever seen him wear other than the occasion appropriate hunting or fishing gear. Blue jeans, flannel shirt, work boots. When I was much younger he used to joke about how his style had finally hit the mainstream with the advent of the 'grunge look'. He didn't say it quite like that though. Bill's mother had died after he got back from Vietnam and his father had left the family when he was still a child. He inherited the small two-story house that was in a neighborhood of South West Portland that had declined with each passing year. He kept the house in good condition despite his neighbors to either side.

He smiled and I went to shake his hand and he tilted his head and smiled bigger and pulled me into his powerful chest and squeezed me to the point it actually hurt. It felt good in a way though and I brought an arm up and around his shoulders and patted his back twice and said, "It's great to see you Bill?" My words were muffled by his giant shoulders covering my mouth. He squeezed even harder and brought my feet six inches off the ground and released me and stepped back and his face was red and his mouth was stretched as wide as it could go.

"Goddamn you've grown up kid. Look at you, all tall and good looking like your old man."

"Thanks, yeah, you're looking good too, Bill."

"Still a little smart ass, like your old man too." He smiled and he roared with laughter and he stepped toward me deliberately like a boxer and picked me up twice as high and twice as hard.

"So where we going anyway, Bill?"

"We're going to get a drink. You're okay with that, aren't you?"

"Of course. Yeah. How have things been going, my dad—"

"Doc says I got cancer, but they ain't no big deal. Just gotta strap myself up to a few machines and shit.

"You're going to be okay though, right? I mean they're treating it?"

"Shit yeah, I'll be fine." I didn't like the way he said it. Bill looked you right in the eyes when he talked to you, almost to the point of making you uncomfortable sometimes, but not this time, not a single word.

"Your dad tells me you've been having some problems."

"What? What'd he say?"

Did he tell you to talk to me or something?"

"Just calm down. He didn't say anything. He just said things have been kind of tough for you since you got back. It's obviously worse than he said though, otherwise you wouldn't be asking like that."

"No. I'm fine. I mean, I don't know. You know how it is."

"I do know how it is. That's why I'm asking you about it now. How bad is it?"

"It's fine. I'm fine. It's just how it is when you get back, I'm fine though." Slowly pulling his just lit unfiltered cigarette from his mouth, he slowed the car down and pulled off to the side of the road and left the lights and engine on. He put his hand on my shoulder and I had no idea what to expect next and was nervous, anxious, excited, and a bit uncomfortable all at once. His eyes were stoic but kind. They shined and looked thick, as though they were made of glass. His skin looked like old worn leather, faint scars from NVA shrapnel peppered the entire left side of his face.

"Drew, I've known you since you were born. Never having any kids of my own, I took to you from the beginning, since you were just a little guy. You know, Drew, whenever I meet somebody new and they ask me if I got kids or not, I tell 'em no, but you're the first thing that pops into my mind when they ask me. For that initial second, I forget you're not *my* son."

He paused and his eyes closed a little and he pushed his baseball cap up away from his eyes with a single thick index finger and continued, but more slowly than before.

"I don't want you to have to go through things the way I did. It doesn't have to be that way for you. But you gotta talk to somebody, Drew. And you gotta find something good to hold on to that can't be touched. You gotta find something new now, Drew; otherwise, it'll rot you; it'll eat away at you until there's nothing left. Don't let it."

Bill hadn't said this many consecutive words in forty years and I felt inadequate but honored that he was spending them on me.

"Now we're gonna go get a drink at the VFW bar. I been coming here every week if not every day since I came back to the states better than thirty damn years ago. There're good folks here, all generations. Everybody's doing something a little different to get by, and you'll see that, Drew; it's what separates the ones that make it when they get back, and the ones that don't. The ones who make it don't forget about it anymore than the ones who don't. Only thing is, the ones who make it find something when they get back worth making it *for*, whatever that is. Figure that out, Drew; whatever it is for you, and grab it with everything you got. And never let go."

I appreciated what he was doing but didn't want to go. I didn't want to think about it anymore than I already had to. It was on my mind enough. I began to sweat as we got closer to the bar. Who would be there, a bunch of old broken soldiers, an unwelcomed glimpse of my inevitable self in thirty years, or maybe less? I didn't know.

The bar was old and from the outside looked like a modular home. It was just off the freeway underneath a crossing overpass so it was very loud. All that marked the front was a rectangular white metal sing that had written across it in red letters, Portland, OR VFW and underneath in smaller black lettering Est. 1947. There was a window on each side with green and yellow neon lights advertising cheap domestic beers. The inside looked like a cross between a WWII bunker and an army recruitment office. Everywhere hung banners of military units, none more prominent than Bill and my respective units, the 101st and 82nd Airborne Divisions. Old black and whites of infantry platoons and helicopter and tank crews were all over the walls. John Wayne posters were everywhere. I ordered a beer from a lanky old man wearing a Marine Corps t-shirt with a large eagle, globe, and anchor tattoo on his right forearm. The tattoo was faded and green and the ink had bled but I could tell what it was because I knew the symbol. His name was Joe. He wore his mustache long and broad like a cowboy and it looked thick and coarse enough to shine a pair of jump boots.

They didn't serve the beer I wanted so I ordered something generic. Neither Bill nor Joe, the bartender, had ever heard of the beer I had wanted and they shared a good laugh saying that "In their day there were only two choices".

I didn't care that they laughed at me. There was a calming relaxation about being the young guy, something I had not felt for a long time. I laughed along with them and ordered whiskey shots for the three of us. Joe respectfully declined and went on to say he hadn't had a drink in fifteen years.

Talking with Bill was like having a conversation with a childhood hero. We spoke of war over several drinks, broadly and philosophically at first, and then tactically, and very specifically. With the passing of each drink, I found myself listening to his accounts more than feeling the need to omit my own. He told me things that he said he hadn't spoken about since they had happened and by the manner in which he expressed them, I could tell he hadn't. It was the first time in a very long time that I had felt genuine pride in something.

I was proud that the man who had taught me so much during my rocky path toward manhood had called on me for what was as much his last confession as it was my first counsel. We both did well from the talk and were half a dozen or so drinks in when a young and loud but kindly energetic drunk man came in.

He shouted out upon his entrance, "Where does the infantry sit?"

And while his forward gesture might have otherwise put me off, I was receptive to his call and answered back, "Right over here, man."

He was an uncommon combat veteran of the first war in Iraq and aged somewhere between Bill and I. He was a portly man, strong looking though, and shaved bald. He wore a biker's vest with every patch and medal he ever earned. He fought with the First Marine Infantry Division and spoke like he was fresher to civilian life than I was.

Taking notice of our similarity in that we fought in the same place just twelve years apart, after a round with the Marine, Bill took up a conversation with Joe the bartender and an older gentleman who looked too drunk to have ever been any kind of soldier.

The Marine and I got along well in conversation because he had a keen ability to strike my still guilty affinity for the infantry with his demeanor that at first reminded me of the good times of it all, without thinking at the moment about the bad. We took our conversation outside over a pack of cigarettes and two pitchers of beer. Even in matters of war, there tends to be a general congregation that naturally occurs between people of a similar age. My fascination with the young Marine had nothing to do with boring company. On the contrary, I hadn't felt more at home since I wore the uniform I ironically couldn't wait to tear off. But I had never talked to anybody about the war like this before, save for a few blacked-out conversations at six-thirty in the morning while on leave.

Like any conversation between a couple of infantry veterans, the talk starts out with stories of barracks sluts, three story beer bongs, and fucked up lieutenants, but those tales are quickly replaced with stories of month long missions, missing limbs, and dying comrades. We were to the point in the conversation where we were sharing our darkes thoughts, but we couldn't remember each other's name.

The question came at me like a spear from the hand of Achilles.

"What's the worst thing you ever did over there?"

It was a question that I had never heard before, thought about every day, yet somehow, I didn't know how to answer. The image was played over in my mind one-hundred times a day since it happened.

I finished the last half of my beer in one long drink, took a deep breath, and said, "On my last tour we were operating in Ramadi, if you know anything about that place."

He nodded his head not wanting to interrupt.

"I was in charge of a truck crew in a delta section. They split the platoon, two trucks to Haditha and two trucks to Ramadi. Anyway, our guys in Haditha were being relieved by some Marines and they came to link up with us in Ramadi for our last mission. We needed the extra gun trucks anyway, so they came along with us but the LT, who was with the other section in Haditha, wanted to be in the lead vehicle on the mission.

Normally, I wouldn't have even given a shit, but I didn't even know this LT. He came to our platoon just a couple of weeks before we left and he had been with the other section the entire tour, so I just didn't trust him. And on top of that, he'd been running missions in Haditha the last six weeks. My guys and I knew Ramadi better than anyone at that firebase. It just didn't make any sense for him to lead."

"So you ended up leading the convoy?" the Marine asked.

"Yeah, and about five minutes out of the wire we got hit by two IED's. My truck got hit in the back end and rolled a few times, we all made it out though. The LT's truck got hit the hardest and he lost both his legs."

"Fuck, man. He made it out though?"

"Yeah, if you wanna call that making it."

"What happened to you guys?"

"We got cut off from the convoy and had to fight our way back to the main body. We all made it out, but the trucks behind us...we lost six guys that night." I said as my words drifted and got quieted to almost a whisper.

"But not ten?" He nearly shouted the words.

"What?"

"You got your men out. It could have been ten dead instead of six."

"Yeah I guess so." I answered hesitatingly.

"So what is it? What was the worst thing then?" He repeated the question like he'd never asked it the first time.

"Well, I mean, that was it I guess. It's the closest I came to dying and losing my men." I could tell by his expression that he was still unsatisfied and wished I had told it differently.

"You feel guilty or something? he asked.

I didn't say anything, afraid that if I said anymore I wouldn't be able to cloak my ambiguous sadness with the confident tone I thought I was projecting, so I just nodded up and down.

"Why?"

He wasn't going to let me off the hook. We were talking about combat, and that's just what we were going to do, talk about *all* of it.

"I don't know. Because I guess it should have been me. It should have been the LT in the front like he wanted. Should have been me I suppose."

"That's a pretty fucked up way to look at things, man. I mean, you got your guys outta the kill zone. Maybe he wouldn't have. You can't ask those kind of questions anyway though. You got your guys out, that's all there is. You did your job, Sergeant."

He said the words like they were completely unquestionable and followed them up with a drink of his beer that took it from half full to empty.

"I think so, yeah, but I'm not doing it now. And neither is the LT, he would have though. Soldiering would have been his life. Now he's got no legs. I was outta there anyway. I was done in the army. He lost a whole career, not just his legs.

"Maybe he was done too. You don't know. Besides, it's not up for you to make sense about why things happened the way they did. Why this guy got hit and this one didn't. Hell, there's a lot worse stuff goes down in country to be worrying about who it could or should have been," he said, while I lit another cigarette and asked if he wanted one.

He hadn't smoked all night but had been staring at my pack for a while and he took one when I asked him. He took a long drag and blew the smoke out from one side of his mouth and then all the way to the other side slowly and said, "During the invasion in '91 I was a lance corporal and a 60 gunner, hadn't fired a shot in combat. We did this patrol outside of some Hajji village. Shit, you know, they all look alike. We nabbed up these two boys who were suspected of assisting Saddam's Guard. We threw these guys in the back of the Humvee. I was on the 60 and we had this weaselly private, named Jenkins, with me in the back. We put a sandbag over Abdul's head and tied his hands and feet. We decided to do the rest of the patrol before we turned him in the command post since we were like ten miles outside the base. We rode around patrolling the streets, questioning whoever acted weird, the sun beating down on our heads the whole goddamn time. You know how fucking hot it gets out there and this guy in the back kept trying to sit up and I'd have to put a boot in his chest and put his ass back down. Fucking Jenkins wasn't doing a goddamn thing to keep control of this guy and after an hour or so I got so pissed off about him moving around in the back that I cracked him in the side of the head with my pistol, damn near knocked him out cold. I told Jenkins to plant his boot in the guy's back and anytime he tried to get up or move, to put his heel right in his spine.

By the time we finished up with our last sector, over three hours had gone by since we picked him up. As we approached the gate on our way back, we got him up off the floor and he was as limp as a fucking sandbag. I kicked him in the ribs, not thinking about what we'd done. He didn't move so I go to cut the sandbag off of his head and a bunch of shit starts dripping out. It smelled like fucking death. We had him face down and I guess he threw up at some point and the sandbag made him choke on it. He was fucking dead. We fucking killed him.

Shit, I didn't know what to do. Jenkins starts freaking out, I mean shit, so was I. I didn't know what else to do so, I told my squad leader that we had to go back to the village. I wasn't really thinking about it; I knew we couldn't just come through the gate with a dead prisoner. We ended up burying him in a huge pile of trash outside the village we just came from. Nobody said anything about it ever again. Nothing ever came of it."

I didn't know what to say to him. Nothing. There was nothing to say. I handed him another cigarette, but he didn't want it. I went inside to get us more drinks. Bill was waiting patiently with the only other person besides the bartender still in the place. I didn't see what the other guy looked like because he was face down on the bar like he was asleep with a half empty beer sitting next to him. It looked like that's how he fell asleep every night. I told Bill what had happened outside, and he shook his head silently and came outside on the patio with me after Joe poured me another pitcher.

"Everything okay out here?" Bill said to the Marine. He was sitting on top of the table with his feet on the chair and leaning his body forward as if he were trying to fold himself in half. I turned to

Bill and told him I thought I should stay but he should go home if he wanted. Bill offered to come pick me up when I was ready, and I told him not to worry about it but he insisted. We hugged. He left and I looked inside and he shook Joe's hand and Joe leaned past his shoulder to look at me outside and smiled and nodded his head and I smiled back at him and waved my hand.

The Marine was sitting straight up now and staring down the empty streets with less expression than a pro poker player. Like most of its citizens, the city had died a little since I remembered it as a kid. I poured us each a beer and giving him a chance to collect himself, I went back inside to get us some whiskey from Joe. When I came back out his posturing was better and he was smoking one of my cigarettes.

I said some cheers that didn't mean anything, and we took our shots and I didn't know if he was going to say anything else for the rest of the night, so I started things off. I could have chosen my subject matter better, but in watching his blank but knowing expression and assuming him around a decade my senior, I was struck with an isolated panic at the idea that he was one of the guys that Bill was talking about who hadn't found his respite from all the horror. I thought of Robertson and was sad in knowing more of why he had done what he had.

"My friend killed himself the other day. We were in Afghanistan together." I didn't know why I told him that.

"You talk to him much?" he asked almost unconcerned.

"I hadn't for a while but then we'd been talking a bunch. Yeah, right before it happened I guess."

"You think there's something you coulda done?"

"I don't know." I said.

"There's nothing you could have done."

"You think we'll go to hell?" I asked.

"*Us?* For what?" He asked with a crooked tone.

"The war." I said.

"Probably." He said.

"Yeah?" I was surprised by his answer.

"Where else would we go?" he asked.

"Heaven maybe," I suggested.

"Heaven?" he asked.

"Well, maybe not heaven," I said.

"I don't know. I heard somebody say once that soldiers don't go to hell. You think God sends soldiers to hell?" he asked like he'd pondered the question many times himself.

"I don't know. I guess He could. What do you think?" I said.

"I think He sends all types there. I imagine it don't much matter a man's profession; if he lived in sin his whole life, he's gonna get what's coming to him."

His words made sense.

"So you think we lived in sin?" I asked.

"Not for me to say. It's all up to him."

He didn't look up but made his hand like a gun as if he were a child shooting at the sky and tipped his empty glass to his lips, taking the last few drops at the bottom.

"I don't think you'll go to hell, man." I said.

I was really trying to save us both.

"Nice of you to say," he said.

"What about me?" I asked.

"What about you?" he asked starkly and gestured for another cigarette.

I gave him one and he used the still lit end of the one he was still smoking to light it.

"You think I will?" I asked.

"Go to hell?" he asked.

"Yeah, you think I'll go to hell?"

My tone reflected my frustration at his increasing hesitancy.

"Not for me to say. Seems about as likely as anybody else I suppose."

His answer was not what I expected. Not that I thought he'd let us off the hook or anything, I just didn't want to be lumped in with all the rest of the sinners I guess.

"What's that supposed to mean?" I asked.

"You know what it means, otherwise you wouldn't be asking me about all this bullshit," he said without looking at me, still staring down the empty night street.

"Well, no. I don't know what you mean actually."

I did know what he meant. I kept picturing Robertson. What was he thinking about before it happened, I wondered. Had he talked to somebody like this before? I wanted to hear it straight out from this Marine. I'd never met somebody like him before and I wanted to hear it straight. No bullshit. He took a drag from his cigarette and flicked it over behind his shoulder and it appeared almost in slow motion, the cherried end cutting through the night's darkness until it reached the ground in an inevitably anticlimactic finish, laying on the ground motionless until it burned out to the butt.

"You killed men. You killed men just like I killed men. Whether those men were trying to kill you or not or what reason we may have had for being where we were, I don't know nowhere where God said that it was okay to kill another man for the reasons we did. We can hide behind all the medals, and flags, and parades, and barbeques in the world and it still don't make any goddamn difference. You and me are killers. That's what we chose to do, plain and simple. And now you want to sit here after its all over and ask me to tell you that we are good men and that God won't judge us for what we've done? I won't do that."

He stood up and put a twenty-dollar bill under his empty glass and walked inside and never came back.

CHAPTER SEVENTEEN
With the Love Parts in Chorus

MY FATHER ONCE TOLD me, in his limited ration of spoken words, "A man cannot change what he has done, only what he will do."

Instead of sneaking vodka from my stashed bottle, I spent the last week smoking some cannabis I had gotten from my friend, Roger, who had recently returned from a backpacking trip around the southern tip of South America. I'd wait until my parents went to bed and then I'd roll a joint in the bathroom, since they were the only rooms in our house with locks. Then I'd go outside on the balcony to smoke it. The past couple of mornings, I smoked what was left of the joint from the night before, and it made me more receptive to the rest of the day.

I had smoked in high school, but not since. I had never experienced it in this new way. It helped me think of things differently. I liked the way that it tasted, and it was easier for me to sit in one place without wondering what was going on in the next room.

Hadley was still at the front of my mind, but I didn't know what else to do with her. All events and participants, both good and bad, from my life were coalescing in some twisted masquerade party inside my confused subconscious and Hadley wandered around amongst them with a familiar ease that always put her at the forefront of those jumbled daydreams. She was always just out of reach though, like some beautiful actress in a movie I was trying to put together in the back of my head. I thought I was a fool to think I could ever have her any other way. We weren't living in a Jane Austin novel. Reality sucks so much most of the time.

I thought of her especially on this day, it being Saturday. Roger always kept really good company. Along with being the first to try cannabis and every other drug, Roger was always the most intellectual of my friends. Kevin was the one who went to college, but Roger was always the smart one. He was never into sports, fighting, cars or any of the other bullshit young American boys waste their time with. He was the only writer I knew, and I hoped that in being around him, whatever artistic qualities he possessed would bring whatever there was of mine to the surface. The more I thought of Hadley, the more I wanted to not just be with her, but be more like her. I think from the very beginning Roger was a way for me to become closer to the person I always wanted to be.

While he was the most artistic person I knew, he spent most of his time smoking and harvesting cannabis. He exhaled so many bong hits while writing his short stories that his computer screen developed a layer of smoke resin so bad that he had to replace it every year. His place was very clean though. He had done well since high school and lived in an apartment downtown near Washington Park, very close to the famous rose gardens. There were houseplants everywhere. Save for the psychedelic rock posters and various maps, the whole place looked like a goddamn rainforest.

My bag of pot from days before was nearly gone. I hadn't been to his new place yet and was interested in seeing it. My parents became skeptical of Roger when we were both in the seventh grade when he came over to our house wearing a Neil Young T-shirt which had a cannabis leaf displayed prominently on the front. My parents were the kind of people who long reserved opinions fostered by such a display and were still weary whilst they hear me speak his name, so I didn't tell them where I was going. I told them I was going to hang out with Kevin, even though we were seeing less of each other the longer I was back.

Roger answered the door wearing a faded black t-shirt with a young black man playing the saxophone on it. His pants were flannel pajama bottoms, a favorite of Roger's for nearly any occasion. His face was clean-shaven as it always was and adorned with a cannabis-induced grin from one ear to the other.

"Hey, what's going on, man?" I said.

"Come here motherfucker, what's all this impersonal bullshit about? Get in here for the real thing."

He threw his arms around me and pulled me into his ambient domicile.

"Come on, sit down, man, just need to finish rolling up this joint real quick. Make yourself at home, brother."

"Your fucking apartment is awesome, man. How the fuck you afford a place so close to the park?"

It really was a beautiful place. A very spacious one bedroom on the twelfth-floor. The view was unbelievable if you could pull yourself away from all the exotic plants enough to actually want to look out a window.

"Business is good, man," he answered, widening his smile even more.

"Looks that way." I replied.

"Yeah, man, blended the strain myself. Try it man, light it up."

He handed me a joint that looked like it had been rolled by a machine, if it rolled joints twice as thick as any cigarette you'd ever seen. Roger wasn't one to waste any time, a quality I always appreciated in a friend.

I took a long drag and held it in as long as I could, enjoying that magic moment when it ignites. The smoke flows down your throat like a warm cloud of comforting joy and it tastes like the earth would if there were no people and everything was pure again. It goes to the back of your throat first and hangs in sweet anticipation for a short but perfect moment before it coats the back of your makes its way over the top of your head and melts forward over your whole body like a euphoric blanket of subliminal hope and radiant brightness. As you blow out the smoke your head evacuates all the day's stress and some of humanity's too. For that moment, and the hour or so that follows, the world is warm, soft, and kind, and you feel as though if things were that way always, you could be the person you dreamed of.

"So yeah man, sorry we didn't get a chance to talk much last time I saw you. Thanks for that weed though, man," I said, with a smile to match Roger's.

"Yeah, any time, brother. Finally got all my shit unpacked and back in order. I been just trying to get all my plants back to where I want them. My neighbor was taking care of 'em for me while I was gone, but it's just not the same if I'm not here with them. I mean don't get me wrong, she's great with them, but she doesn't sing to them or anything."

He spoke of his plants as if they were his children, and to Roger, they very much were.

"Well they look great, man. Maybe I should have gotten into this instead."

I was half waiting for Roger to say something in regard to my comment, but he just smiled even wider and said, "Yeah, man, so you liked that herb I hooked you up with then? You smoked it all up already, so you must have."

"Oh, it's great man. Yeah, it's pretty much gone. Way better than any of that shit we smoked in high school," I said.

"Glad you liked it. Yeah, a lot's changed since high school." he replied.

"Not for some people it seems like," I said.

"Yeah, no shit. That reminds me, Kevin said you been hanging out with some of the old crew. How's that been going man?" he asked, taking another slow long drag from the burning joint.

"Those fucking guys. I see why you moved up here," I said.

"Yeah, man. I'd seen enough in high school. Kevin said something about you not really getting along with them too well," he said.

"Yeah, I can't stand those guys. Kevin's fine and all you know, but the rest of those guys, it's just all so simple for them, you know what I mean?" I asked rhetorically knowing well that Roger knew exactly what I meant.

"Oh yeah, man. They got nothing to say but what they want to eat and fuck. Very base for those types. Shit gets real tired, real quick," he said.

"Not for them though I guess," I said.

"Yeah but at least Kevin's back in town and you can get a place with him. That'll be cool, right?" he asked.

"Well yeah, man. Kevin and I still get along just fine, I mean, you know, it always was the three of us really, the rest of those guys were mostly just there. The only reason we were friends with the rest of those guys is because we all grew up next to each other. Funny how that works when you're young," I said with a fake little chuckle.

"Yeah, dude, I feel ya. You know a part of me will always love Jason and those guys but meeting up for them every couple of months or so is about it for me now. Shit, I haven't even seen anybody but you and Kevin since I've come back. Just different interest now is all. Anyway, man, Kevin tells me you been going to Strega for poetry readings."

"Yeah, man. Met a girl there too. Well, kind of. She's got a boyfriend," I answered.

"Shit man, that's never stopped the Drew Hoskins I know."

I didn't like hearing that but knew he meant it in jest. It bothered me only because it was true. But whatever confidence I had once possessed had been replaced by another kind of confidence that kept me alive in battle. Strangely, these are of a different type and one in no way contributes to the other.

"And you met her in there at Strega?" he asked.

"Yeah, they were doing their open mic thing. I was trying to get away from all the fraternity guys that were out prowling the streets for drunk girls," I said.

"Oh yeah, no shit, man. Those fucking wine walks and beer crawls and all that shit; they're just goddamn date rape buffets for those fucking fraternity animals. You don't wanna fuck with any of those girls out there anyway man. Trust me," he said, handing me the joint.

"Oh, I know, I know. I learned my lesson young at least."

Roger had warned Kevin about Sarah when he dated her in high school. And then after, when she left, Roger warned me.

"Let's not even go down that road. Just glad you finally got away from that fucking parasite. You got better things ahead, brother. That reminds me, a few days ago you said you were going to start school. That's gotta be really soon, right?" he asked with excitement.

"Yeah man, starts in just a few weeks," I said.

"And they'll pay for all your shit; the Army, right?" he asked.

"Oh, yeah. I mean, I got the GI Bill and all, so I figure I may as well go," I said.

"Fuck yeah dude, go get your learn on. What are you thinking about majoring in, or are you even thinking about that yet?" he asked.

"Actually, yeah, quite a bit really," I said.

"Yeah, what are you thinking?" he asked.

"English probably, you know literature or something," I said, waiting for his reaction.

"Fuck yeah, dude. If you're going to spend the time and money on school, you should do something you want to do," he said.

"That's what Kevin was saying too," I replied.

"Shit man, he would know. He's going for his masters and shit this fall. Fucking scholar and a gentleman, know what I'm saying?"

"You don't think you'll ever go?" I asked.

"No, man," he said without hesitation.

"It seems like it would be kind of your thing, you know?"

I didn't want to push, but always wondered why Roger never went to school.

"Na, man," he answered and handed the joint back to me without saying anything else.

"But you were always the smart one of us, man. Shit, you still read more books than anybody I know," I said.

"Maybe, that's all different though."

I could tell Roger didn't want to say anything else about it, but I respected his opinion very much and wanted to know why one of the smartest and most inquisitive people I had ever known had chosen to not continue his formal education after high school.

"It just seems like it'd be so easy for you, you already do more reading and stuff than anybody who goes to college," I said.

"Well first off, don't get me wrong, I think college can be great and I'm super proud of Kevin for all he's done. That kid knows some shit and can talk it too. And I'm really stoked that you're gonna go man, I know you'll do well. But for me, I just can't get into it, man. School never was my thing. I just had to do well or my parents would ground me. You know how that was, man."

As he spoke, he gazed into the lit end of the joint in my hand as if encapsulated by its burning light.

He paused for a moment and continued on, "For me I think it's just that I feel like I can't learn the way people want me to, or at least it's just not the way it works best for me. Take all these plants for example, man."

He took the joint from my hand and relit the end and took a long drag in and exhaled the smoke while he pointed around the room. Like I said before, the place looked like a goddamn rainforest.

He took another long drag and spoke while the smoke escaped his moving lips, "I got into plants really hard the summer right after we graduated. It was right after Stacy just cheated on me with that U of O dickhead. You'd already left for boot camp. At first it was really easy to grow everything, but then I wanted to expand out and start growing different tropical plants and shit like that so I took a botany class at the community college, so I could learn more about what I was doing. Well, about halfway through the semester, I got so wrapped up into all the shit the professor was teaching us and trying to do things the way they were teaching them, that my plants were all practically dead. I finished out the class and by the time it was over I had a ninety-eight percent and not one plant still alive. It took me the rest of the fall to replant everything I had lost. By just going to the library and looking shit up on the internet for free, I got my garden to look like this, and now I grow the best product in the entire city. Completely locally sourced. Urban gardens will be the future of the industry, brother."

He pointed around the room again, this time using the joint instead of his finger and then he handed it to me and said, "I gotta learn things my own way, man, that's all." I wish I had the discipline that you and Kevin have, believe me, man."

What Roger didn't realize was that he was the one with the real discipline.

"Yeah, man. You're exactly right. See that's the problem with it, man. That should be what college is. This should be what it is right here, what you and I are doing, just talking, man. Fuck paying thousands of dollars to go to school with a bunch of people who have never had an original thought in their sheltered lives. I mean, why even go to college anyway?"

I could get carried away into a conversation really quickly when I was as high as I was. Roger didn't mind though.

"To get that certificate, man. Gotta get that paper. Isn't that why you're going?" he said.

"Shit, I don't know, man. I don't know why *I'm* going. I'm going so I don't have to get a job. I don't know, maybe I can read some good shit along the way and write my own book someday or something. Or maybe I'll just move to Milan. I really don't know."

I felt stupid listening to what I was saying but I felt stupid like a teenager might feel stupid, it didn't slow me down for one minute.

"Milan?"

"Yeah. Always wanted to go there. Maybe I should just say fuck it and go there."

"I'd go to Milan."

"Fuck'n A right, dude."

"Let's go." he said as he put precision smoke rings into the air. And I could tell that Roger, seasoned as he was, was just as high as me.

"You wanna go?" I asked, this time as though it were a real possibility.

"What's here anyway, man? I mean, it's pretty clear that the whole 'work hard and do well in school and it will all pay off' promise we all got from our parents, teachers, and everybody goddamn else, was nothing more than a bullshit illusion of what they were going to hand to their kids. But they forgot that we didn't have the privilege of growing up in a glorified national backdrop of saving the world in WWII and putting the first man on the moon."

He handed the joint back to me and started pacing around the coffee table in his living room. He took a deep breath in and started back into his diatribe.

"We came from angry and confused Vietnam veterans, man. We came from empowered woman who were still getting their asses pinched in the office. We watched *Predator* and *Terminator,* Desert Storm on TV, man. And now we're grown up and it's time for us to have our own kids and careers and wives. But people don't get married anymore and we can't afford to have kids because we don't have careers because they're still running the same old machines. That's our fuckin' story. The kids of the non-elite, born between the years of *their* lord 1975 to1990."

I looked down at the joint that had gone out and instead of lighting it I stared into its burned-out end as Roger spoke with a passion I hoped I'd someday have. He took the joint from out of my hand and relit it. Roger didn't need me to say something good back. Roger didn't need anybody to say anything for him to just keep on talking about that kind of stuff. I liked to listen to him too. Nobody else talked the way he did. He paused and smiled at me before starting up again.

"We think we're so fucking smart too, people, like we've got it all figured out." He laughed through his nose, took a slow breath in and looked and me and said, "You know that people have really only been out of the jungle for five or maybe ten thousand years, man. You ever think about that, man? Modern humans have been here for only around two hundred thousand years. So, we've only been living in civilization for less than one percent of our existence as a species. You ever think about that, man?"

He repeated and waited for me to respond and I spoke of the only thing I knew much about. "It just seems like it will always be this way. It always has been," I said.

"Like what?" he asked. He really wanted to know what I thought.

"You know. Just people killing each other. And I don't just mean here and there, but on the big fucking scale, wars and shit. It's just always happened," I said.

Roger sat down on the edge of the couch where I was and said, "I know what you mean man, I mean, not like you I'm sure, I've never been to war obviously, but I know what you mean about us always killing each other. But it doesn't make sense when you think about it, man, why we kill each other I mean. It seems to me that it's like a herd mentality thing because people aren't willing to fight and kill each other like that anywhere else. I mean there's always going to be some people who will kill each other, crazy people and murderers and shit like that but what is it that makes people want to kill people that they've never met. People who they would have had no problem with if some politician on TV wasn't telling them they should?"

"I guess they're just afraid. I don't know. I guess I was. Not afraid of them, or any kind of enemy, or at least I wasn't. But I was afraid of not being a part of it I guess. Like being back on the playground as kids or something when one of your friends starts a fight with a group of other kids and you have to go in and fight too. Not because you have to protect your friends, just so you don't look like you were afraid of getting hurt."

"You think you'll ever write about the war, man?" he asked, and the joint had gone out and all the wind from our voices had escaped with it.

"I've had some ideas since being back. Things are just so much different than I imagined them. The world's got a lot faster since I've been gone, and it seemed to forget about the war sometime along the way. I'll never forget it though, and that's what bothers me I guess. For everybody else, it's just this thing that they see on the news and talk about after they see some soldier singing the national anthem at a football game or something, but they don't actually consider what's going on or why that soldier is fighting. It's funny, I've heard old people say that, 'Youth is wasted on the young,' but I think my youth was wasted on their war."

"You're right, brother. Nobody really thinks about what you guys are losing when you're over there, what we're all losing really. You should tell your story. I think you could do it in a way that would really make people listen, and understand maybe a little bit better about what they're supporting."

"People don't want to hear what I have to say about it. They just want to hear about how honorable and brave we all were. How we endured the hardships of combat together with the pride of defending American freedom and making the world safe for democracy. They don't want to hear about what it was really like; about what we were really doing over there."

"No. Most people don't want to hear about that stuff. But they need to. I'm just saying that I think you would be the perfect one to tell his story. I don't want to bum you out, man. I know what you mean. I wouldn't want to write about that stuff either if I were you."

"The fucked up part though man, that's the only stuff I can really remember, all the fucked up shit. Everything I remember enough to write about is from combat. It's like it's the only part of my life I really lived. The rest of it's like a faded picture. I just don't know how to get the rest of it back, man"

"Go take it back, Drew. Or at least make something new. Yeah, man. Do that." Roger stood up and was smiling wide again as he relit the joint and put it in the corner of his mouth. He looked at me like he was going to give me a hug and said, "Get new shit, man, better shit that makes you smile when you think about it. That's the thing about life, the really good parts don't happen nearly often enough, and when they do, they don't last nearly long enough either. You need way more of those moments, man, you deserve them, we all deserve them. The best parts of life should last way longer, you know? Like your favorite meal, a great book, falling in love, it's all over way too quickly. The best parts of life should be long and hard-hitting and repeat over and over again like a great rock 'n' roll song. That's how it should be, man. That's how we all need to live, with the love parts in chorus."

CHAPTER EIGHTEEN
Out with the Old in with the New

THAT CONVERSATION WITH ROGER played over and over again in my mind until it all finally made perfect sense. It's funny how you can hear just the right thing for the first time, and even though you don't quite get it yet, you can fall in love with the idea like it's the answer to all of existence. Roger had always had a way of saying things in just the right way to make you think he was the greatest genius who ever lived. But the more I thought about what he told me, the more he became like a sage, ensconced in the green shrubbery of the only thing that was sacred to him. He knew how to separate what he loved, and he knew how to hold it apart from the rest of the world so that it could be pure and free to grow in whatever way he and the universe together decided.

There was more to learn from that single conversation than there was from the tongue of any scholar or holy man. And as I contemplated Roger's words, I became keenly aware of my own salvation. War had been hard, but I was alive and the only way to reconcile those two facts was to learn. I didn't want to be like that Marine. I didn't want my mom to find me at the end of a rope or next to a bottle of pills like Robertson. Admirable as he was, I didn't even want to end up like Bill or the bartender who served us. These were all good men and had fought with the same vigor, and I fear eventual regret, as I once had. Long nights like these turn too easily into long years and then decades and then lifetimes. If there was going to be something that separated me from them, it was up to me to make that separation happen right then. I had to let go of all the things that still took me back to that night in Iraq.

A strange accompaniment to the enlightened perspective I was granted came as naturally and unexpectedly as the clarity I then saw. While realizing fully what Hadley truly meant to me, I was also stuck with a harsh sense of my own dull stupidity that I have carried with me to some degree every day forward. I knew nothing about the world. I knew of war. I knew of death. But I knew nothing of life, of love. I knew nothing of poetry or art or of science or sex. I wanted to know more. I wanted to know everything. Mostly, I wanted to know Hadley. It had taken Whitman and Wolfe, my mom and my dad, Kevin, Roger and Robertson, that old shit covered paratrooper and the Marine and Bill and the bartender and everybody in between that I didn't notice at the time to teach me what I could never have learned by myself. There are some things in life that stay with us. They are different for everyone, but they stick all the same. It's not about what happened or for how long or to what degree that makes us different. What makes us different is how hard we let those things bite at us, and how much we let those bites fester, and for how long, and how deep. It had come time to leave the black.

I thought back to the second time I'd met Hadley and we talked about Hemingway and what she'd said about him. How he had to rewrite reality for himself. I didn't want to be like that. I wanted to have my own story, apart from all the long drunken nights with cheap bottles of liquor. Hadley was as much a way of life as she was a tangible being. I loved her long before I ever had the chance to truly know her. And as I became more and more acquainted with the person underneath the splendid allure, a special satisfaction fell upon me for recognizing my guiding light that Bill and Roger had told me to go find.

Graceful as she was, her words carried the message of some-body like me. Somebody not lost, but abandoned, and not by any one person, but by her own idealism. The world was strange and dark in most of its places and the more I had seen outside of war, the more I understood that these nasty stings life throws at us with such abundance are rationed at a more or less equal amount from birth. Favor and riches take a person far in substance but nowhere in constitution. And for those like Hadley and Roger and my parents and even Kevin, existence, no matter how sweet at times, would always be battered by those relentless spoilers of taste and life and wisdom and love.

College registration was a few days away and I was, for the first time in my life, eager for class. Not for what it was, but what it could be; something new, something I didn't know. It meant possibility, and that was enough to excite me. Mostly though, it brought my mother and me as close together as we had ever been. She was the sort who loved her child regardless of his reason or reservation, but it brought a great comfort to her expression that I had not seen in many years, that I was taking an interest in the same things that she once had held so dear. And in discussing the rigors of figuring out for oneself what is truly right, she espoused words that made me think I had been waiting all these years for the wrong parent to speak.

We went to lunch together at a Mexican restaurant that was my favorite as a kid. The neighborhood was very poor, and I noticed the difference much more now than as a child. There was a white man and woman with two young boys who sat next to us. The children were loud, and the man was very rude to the young waitress. His wife seemed embarrassed but subdued. My mother did not look over at them but sighed and looked into my eyes and smiled. Her eyes watered a bit and she said how happy she was that I was home. She put her hand on top of mine and told me how much she loved me, and I told her that I loved her. We talked about college and she said that regardless of how much it would help me professionally, I would gain things that are beyond any monetary value.

"Left alone, Drew, we'd all grow up to be cold and cruel to each other. We have to learn and to be taught and actually *want* to understand that we're all unique in our own small little ways, but all that matters is that we're all sharing in the same experience. We all see the same sun in the day and the same moon and stars at night. We speak different languages and pray to different gods, but we all love our children and just want better lives. It's just too easy and too, I think maybe even instinctual, for us to live like we're going at it alone and thinking that helping others only hurts ourselves. But people are only as good as how much work they've put into being good, Drew. Compassion and empathy are learned attributes, Drew, just like typing or even shooting a gun. If a person makes bad decisions that hurt other people, it's because they haven't learned enough to understand that their actions truly hurt people." I wanted that to be true and it sounded so good, but I wasn't sure.

"I just don't know. I mean I think that can be true, but it's just, I don't know, it seems to me like everybody talks about compassion and understanding and empathy and everything, but when it comes right down to it, those things are just words. People don't just help other people, not when they have to actually put themselves out to do it, I don't think." I took a sip from the end of my straw and waited for me mother's response.

"You did, Drew." She said with a small smile.

"I did what?" I asked confused.

"You put yourself out to help people. When you were only 17 you decided to do that, you risked your life for that in fact." She said it very proudly, sitting back in her seat, straight and upright like a soldier, but still with a subdued smile.

"Yeah, that wasn't for me though, Mom, you know that."

"I don't know that. I don't even believe that." Her expression hadn't changed.

"Well, it's true."

"Why did you join then, Drew?" She asked.

"I think I just wanted to be a part of something that was bigger than myself. I mean, I was only 17. I just wanted to prove myself. I didn't even know what I was doing." I said.

"You knew what you were doing. Maybe you didn't know what it was going to be like, but you knew what you were doing." She said.

"Why do you think I joined?" I asked.

"I used to wonder that every single day, and until you left, I'd hoped that you would change your mind. You obviously never did. I remember when you started getting ready to sign up, you were doing pushups every day and running all the time to get ready, watching war movies every night, it's all you talked about your senior year, Drew. I was proud of you already, but I didn't understand it all."

"Why were you proud then? I interrupted.

"Well, I think that you showed a maturity that I'd never seen in you before. I'd never really seen it in anybody that young. You really wanted to be there, to fight the war, and we all thought that was noble cause at the time. I was scared for you every day, Drew, even before you left because I saw what happened to all our boys in Vietnam. I didn't want that for you, but I knew that you did. I certainly wasn't going to try and talk you out of it. It'd just convinced you that you were right in wanting to go in the first place, you never did listen to your poor ol' mom, Drew, and now I have this whole head of gray hair." She reached her hand out to meet mine and continued. "I love you so much, Drew, and I've always been proud of you. I know things are very hard right now, and I wish more than anything that I could do something to make it better."

"Things are better, Mom." I said, trying to seem genuine and confident in my words.

"I remember when Bill came back from Vietnam. Your dad was so excited to see him. He didn't know that any of his friends or anything were going to meet him when he came in, but his mom called your dad up as soon as she heard so we could all go to greet him together. You know how your dad is, he never wants to show it, but he was so excited for him to be home, not as excited as he was before we went to pick you up, but close. Anyway, that was when you could actually go out on the runway to meet people as they landed and got off the plane. We were all out there like in the movies, lined up, your dad and a couple of his other friends, Bill's mom and his two sisters and I think Bill's cousin was there too. We'd made an American flag pattern on a sign with his name written over it, and a big, 'Welcome Home'. Your dad was so excited when he finally landed and he saw him walking off the plane, that he forgot to even hold up the sign, so there I am, trying to hold this gigantic sign that your dad and I made the night before and he's just bouncing around like a kid on Christmas." She laughed as she said it.

"I can't even imagine seeing Dad like that ever."

"Well, it was so sad, Drew. Bill came walking down the stairs and I know he saw us because we were directly in front of him, but he didn't look excited or anything, in fact, he had the blankest face I'd ever seen, I remember it like it was yesterday. Bill was always the stoic type, even when we were really young, but this was different, he was different. He walked right past us. His mom didn't say anything and looked down the line at your Dad and I who were confused as to what to do. Bill's mom just put her hand up and motioned it softly up and down as if to gesture that it was alright, to just let him keep going." She took a drink of her soda and stopped as though that might be all to the story.

"Where'd he go? What did you guys do?" I asked leaning forward.

"We just kind of followed slowly behind him. He grabbed his bag and walked through the parking lot until he found his mom's car. It was really weird, like he knew right where it would be or something. He walked right up to it, put his duffel bag on top of the trunk and turned around and leaned against the car facing us as we approached him with hesitation. His mom stopped us all and asked if we wanted to just meet them back at the house. You dad was heartbroken I think. I went up to Bill and he looked at me like he was going to stop me from coming any closer, I almost stopped because I had no idea what I was going to actually say to him, but I kept walking forward and he leaned up away from the car and said, 'Glad you two made it, Kate.' I took one more step forward and put my arms out slowly and he looked at each of my hands, as if to check if I were holding something. He leaned into me and we hugged and he hid his face in my shoulder. You know, Bill was never much taller than me; I could feel him crying. We stood there for a moment and then his mom and sister came up. When he lifted his head from my shoulder, he had no tears in his eyes; he was stoic Bill again. He said, thanks for coming here everybody. And he opened the car door and got in and didn't say more than twenty words the rest of the night."

What the hell was she doing teaching math all those years, I thought to myself. I was happy though that she had the chance now to talk about these things again, and I felt more like a son than ever before in that it was me who she spoke with.

We ordered fried ice cream with strawberries for desert. We somehow ended up talking about the war and I found the clearest words I had ever spoken on the subject fell from my mouth like they had always wanted to. "All wars are the same in most ways probably. What Grandpa did in WWII and what Bill did in Vietnam wasn't much different than what we did in Iraq or Afghanistan. But I think it gets worse each time. Not the fighting necessarily, I mean just the war itself, the nastiness of it all. I think each new war is kind of worse than the last because it's just one more war on top of another on top of another, it makes the last one seem kind of pointless and it makes everything that happened seem like it's in vain, like we're dying for no reason or something. I mean, I did three separate tours, and each time I went, it got worse, the fighting was worse, the relationships with the locals were much worse, and even though our side learned a lot from the early years of the war, it began to feel like we were losing. It just didn't matter what we did, how many people we killed, the war was going to go on anyway just the same. When I left for Afghanistan, I felt like Grandpa going to fight the Nazis, but now, I mean fuck, Mom, I think maybe Bill had as much reason to fight in Vietnam as I did Iraq. I just don't know what we did there, or even in Afghanistan really."

She understood much of what I told her. What she didn't understand was impossible, her maintaining the same reserved idealism for not only the outcome of humanity, but even more particularly the conduct of our home nation, that so many of her generation inevitably cling to. I don't blame her or anybody else for holding a partiality toward their own country though. Denigrating to our elders as we might appear to be, I believe the lion's share of the Millenials' problem with our parent's and grandparent's generation is not so much in the decisions they made that fostered the current conditions, but more with the dwelling attitude and apathetic labels that have been unfairly assigned to us in the aftermath of those societal misfortunes we have been forced to endure. But I don't want to go on to talk about what my generation had to go through that the last didn't and what the next one won't. I'm not a brilliant man, however, I have enough faculties to surmise that every generation fancies themselves more hard working than the current and more dignified than the last, so I won't indulge in the temptation of generational attack and defense any more than I already have.

My personal experiences, and therefore subsequent philosophy, is based upon a tradition no more original than generational bickerings. What I know and believe of the world was established and will therefore always to some degree be rooted in the philosophy of battle. My musings and philosophical ponderings are bread from the bloodied ground that we seem destined to return to generation after generation. And if for no other reason than our relentless return to killing and dying, we are all at least as foolish as the last.

I was a soldier once though and for however long ago that would be, it was to a degree that makes my body, and too often mind, think we're still in the thick of battle. While I was a soldier I had created another world. Since coming back, that world seemed even further away. For when in battle, it was possible because of its intangibility. Now that it was tangible, I knew it was never real. But I had needed that world once, we all did. One we all created from our watchtowers and while on long foot patrols though forests, jungles, mountains, desserts and cities. It's a world beyond the wire and beyond the war and beyond anything we knew before. It was different for everybody, but we all knew it the same. For some it was filled with riches and houses, and boats and political power. For others it was as simple as fine drink and beautiful women. Life is about two things, as I heard from a Virginia born paratrooper, "cold beer and warm pussy". That world we created on long nights and early mornings was never really there though and this is what my mom didn't understand. It wasn't just the cell phones and computers and cable TV, it was a whole new world. Not of bravery, but of brevity. We were living in a time that was akin for the nonconformist to the experiences of the Beat Generation. It was a cold and dusty time when the cigarette smoking leather jacket wearing cool guy was demonized and blind obedience and night-stick violence was praised. A time when Eleanor Roosevelt is remembered as hard-featured instead of illustriously noble. Those of us who are disenfranchised by the ever-decaying social ambiance of modern America and disobedient to the social standards of consumerism and the commands of jingoist propaganda are cast to the fringes of an increasingly fascist police state. We have made our homes on the outer crust and have been desperately gnawing away at it ever since. And we will continue to bite and to chew and to scratch our way back to dignity or to death. It was a very different time than what my mother and her generation were used to. We had the same spirit of the kids in the 60's, that's what they didn't understand, but when they all stopped, the opposition fortified, and they were now more powerful than ever. This is what we came home to. This was our post war dream.

CHAPTER NINETEEN
Yellow Ribbons and White Flags

BY SUMMER'S END I was a regular at Strega. It was why I left my house. The event had drawn me every week and the bartenders didn't ask me what I wanted to drink anymore. That the event was a weekly poetry reading placed me somewhere between an anxiety ridden infantry veteran and the everyday hipsters that festered in the scene of any contemporary city scene. I had gotten to know most of the regular participants to the point of knowing most of their names and preferred drinks. Hadley was no exception, but while I was at least satisfied by my level of association with every other poet, I was completely *un*satisfied with that of mine and Hadley's.

Hadley normally carried a causal happiness to her disposition that was noticeably absent on that day. She did not test the microphone with the usual one finger tap I had seen her do every other time. She never looked up from the paper. She didn't say her name. All she said was, "This isn't my poem, but I wanted to read it because it's very true to me. It's called 'May' and it's by Sara Teasdale."

> *The wind is tossing the lilacs,*
> *The new leaves laugh in the sun,*
> *And the petals fall on the orchard wall,*
> *But for me the spring is done.*
> *Beneath the apple blossoms*
> *I go a wintry way,*
> *For love that smiled in April*
> *Is false to me in May*

The audience was less busied than they usually were and the silence of their attention was broken only as she left the stage, sending the room into a soft applause. I remained standing just inside the doorway like I usually did if I were by myself. A young man and woman approached Hadley as she stepped down from the stage. I was too far away to hear what they said to her, but it made Hadley smile and I was glad they were there. The bartender announced that there was a break in the readings after Hadley finished and all the people congregated at the bar for another drink or outside on the porch for an early evening cigarette. Hadley was still talking to the young couple and looked over at me and mouthed the word 'hi'. I put my glass in the air and nodded my head and gave a small smile. They both hugged her before the conversation ended. When Hadley walked toward me, the bar was all but empty inside. It had been very crowded before but now there were just a couple of people sitting on the edge of the stage drinking beer. The bartender put on some old delta blues and announced that there would be a few more readings later on in the night but to drink up in the meantime.

There was less movement in her shoulders and hips than usual. She tried to smile as she came closer and did but it was small, and I knew not altogether real and it made me sad to see.

Not knowing what else to do or say, I asked, "Do you want me to go get you a drink?"

"Thanks. I'm okay. I don't much feel like it right now." We sat down at a table outside and the wind started to blow lightly but felt good because the day had been very hot.

"Just let me know if you want me to get you anything," I said.

"Thanks, Drew." She said without looking directly at me.

She brushed some strains of dangling curls from the right side of her face with two straightened fingers and her mouth sagged some at the corners.

"More people than I'm used to this week." she added while looking into the bar and focusing on nothing in particular.

"That's what I was thinking too. That's good though. It's good to see people are coming out," I said.

"I remember when they first started doing these things. I was a sophomore I think." She paused and looked over at me from the side for a short moment and then turned her face toward me and her eyes were not as sad as her mouth., "Three years ago when I first came. I think there were about six of us here, including the bartender."

"At least some people still like stuff. I was talking with my mom the other day about coming here to the readings, and she was all excited that they still have stuff like this. I guess her and my dad used to go to stuff like this a bunch when they were young."

"That's cool that you talk to your parents about stuff like that. You must be pretty close with them then?" she asked.

We'd never talked about our families.

"Yeah. I mean, not really, sometimes, I guess, kind of, you know. I'm staying with them right now until Kevin and I get a place. I don't know, it's been different since I came back."

"Yeah. I imagine. Was your dad ever in the army or anything?" she asked.

"No. But he acts like he was sometimes. I mean, he's not all militant or anything like that, just really serious most of the time," I said.

"Is your mom like that too?" she asked.

"She is most of the time. They're happy though. They just have their own way about things I guess. I think things change maybe as you get old together. I mean, they've been together since they were younger than we are now," I said.

"That's really special though. When two people can still be together and love each other after that long."

Her eyes widened as they normally were as she said it, but only for that instant, as if she needed only a moment to realize she'd lost something.

"Yeah, I think it's a different kind of love though. You know? I don't think that they're *in* love anymore," I said.

"I don't know them obviously, but I bet they're still in love, it just looks different than somebody our age thinks it should look like." She said. I just smiled at her and she smiled back at me and asked, "What is it?"

"Oh, nothing, I'm just happy to be here I guess." I said.

"I'm really glad you came today, you wanna get that drink?" She said as she was standing.

As we stood in line I imagined that she was my girlfriend. I hoped that people thought she was my girlfriend. I loved just standing next to her waiting for beer. We could have been anywhere, waiting for anything, even socks, it was perfect because she was there.

When we got back outside, Hadley, for whatever reason, decided she was going to let me know a big part of her that I didn't.

"So, you moved here for school, right?" I asked her.

"Yeah, a little over four years ago now," she said.

"And you like it, obviously," I said.

"I do. I didn't much at first, but I do now," she said.

"What changed for you?" I asked.

"Just the way I looked at it really. I came here for school, but more than anything else I came here to escape. I didn't like where I was, and I thought that anywhere in the world would be better than Cleveland. I built up Portland to be this like special refuge for the spirited but disenfranchised youth. It sounds pretty stupid now when I think about it, but I thought it was going to be like San Francisco in the late '60s or something like that when I came out here. I was pretty depressed I guess when it wasn't, and all the rain didn't help either."

She took a long drink of her beer and looked at me like she was trying to figure something out and then continued on and the corners of her mouth now pointed up a bit when she spoke.

"It is special here. You have to want to be a part of it though, you have to let yourself be affected."

"Yeah, yeah, you're right about that, that is what it is. I think that's what I'm trying to do right now. I had a plan too, I guess. Well, not a plan, but an idea; some daydream that I somehow convinced myself was real about the way things should be when I got out of the army."

"You probably needed that when you were over there. I mean, how else would you get through all that? But then you have to come home and realize that it's not all that great on the other side either. I mean, no wonder so many veterans have problems when they come home," she said.

Hadley listened to everything I said, actually heard me. I'd never known what that was like before then.

"I think that's a big part of it for sure," I said as I reached for a cigarette. I lit one and continued, "It's not just what went on over there that messes with people's heads, it's what happens to them when they get home that can really screw 'em up too. I don't know, we all have things we're going through though. Just seems like people forget that way too easily. You know, that we all have things we're fighting through."

"But not you, Drew Hoskins."

"What? What do you mean?"

There was a crack in my voice that was more induced by panic than excitement and I had no idea what she meant.

"You. *You* don't forget that stuff. That everybody's fighting something. Most people do, Drew. You should be proud of that."

She drank the rest of her beer and leaned forward, putting her elbows on the table and her face close to mine but not looking right at me but to the side, at the street.

"Paul didn't get it. He really didn't. He seemed like a really great guy. And he was most all the time, but it just wasn't ever very real. You know what I mean? He was always polite and all that, but I don't think he really cared what other people went through or what they felt about life or how it affected them. It's easy for people like him, so he thinks it's that way for everybody else too. But it isn't.

You understand that, Drew. I can already tell that about you. Paul didn't get it. Most people don't get it."

"Is that what it was? I mean is that all that happened with him?" I asked.

"There were other things. I didn't love him," she said.

I rejoiced.

"I'm sorry, I didn't mean to bring anything like that up," I said.

"Oh no; its totally fine."

But she looked as though she were fighting back tears and I put my hand on top of hers which laid on the table with her fingers curled under her palm. She looked down at our hands and I could feel her breath stop and she looked up at me and did not smile but her eyes didn't look sad like they were before. She turned her hand over and our palms pressed together and then she turned her hand back over so mine was again on top of hers.

"He didn't love me either. It was better this way," she said.

"I'm sure he loved you Hadley." But not like I would. I thought to myself.

"He thinks he did. And I know he wanted to most of the time. But he couldn't. I don't blame him though. I couldn't ever really love him either. It's funny how you can live your life next to somebody for so long and after all of it you can look at each other like you don't share one common experience. That's how it was with Paul and me," she said and chuckled without smiling or moving her lips.

There was always a softness to Hadley, whatever she was feeling. Whether it be joy or sorrow there was always a little of the other mixed in and it made her graceful, and more beautiful than anything I had ever watched be.

We drank together for the next couple of hours. More precisely, Hadley, myself and whoever invited themselves into our conversation, drank together for the next couple of hours. I was glad I was keeping her distracted and relatively happy. I knew she never loved Paul, but I knew that did not altogether matter. Whenever somebody loses a lover, no matter what the circumstances or who the initiator, it is a sad and lonely time because we have lost somebody who knows us in a way that most others will not. Regardless of the level of the association, something is shared between lovers that cannot ever be replaced, and this is felt more especially when both are young and have not had as many lovers.

It had gotten dark, the air had cooled, and Hadley covered her shoulders with a navy-blue cardigan that she left unbuttoned and did not put her arms through. There was a couple sitting next to us. They were having a good time at first and were loud but had become quiet as the evening prolonged. The poets were all done and had been for a while. The music was a mix of big band and bop jazz and people were talking over it in pairs and small groups. The porch was filled with smokers and drinkers and a group of four young college age men who sounded like they were only minutes away from turning their verbal altercation into a physical one but nothing happened as it usually didn't. I asked Hadley what had brought her to Portland and she laughed a little and asked me if I had ever been to Cleveland. I had not.

"You go back and visit much?" I asked her.

"Haven't been back since my sophomore year." Her words quickened.

"It's been over three years. Damn. I mean, that's fine. Are you not close to you family, or...?"

"No. I was with my mom. But nobody else really," she said.

"Does she not live there anymore?" I asked.

"She died almost four years ago," she said.

"My god. I'm sorry. I had no idea."

I hated my response. People always say that when they bring up something troubling on accident like that, *"Oh, I had no idea".* Of course you had no idea; doesn't change the fact that you said it one bit though.

"It's okay. We haven't talked about it at all. I forget sometimes that we haven't known each other long. Yeah, she died right before I started my second year of college. My parents divorced when I was fourteen. I haven't seen my dad since then," she said.

"I'm sorry. That must be really hard. I complain way more than I should," I said.

"Not at all, Drew. I can't imagine going through what you did. But yeah, it is hard, but it's my choice. It's the way I want it. He still wants to see me. He didn't abandon us or anything."

"What happened?" I asked.

"My mom got pancreatic cancer when I was in junior high and had to go through surgery. Then it spread and she had to have chemo and all that. She made it, but it was a really hard time for all of us. I guess my dad started seeing some woman he worked with when it didn't look like my mom was going to make it. I always tried to tell myself that he only did it because he thought for sure that she was going to die, and he wouldn't be able to handle it when it happened, so he found somebody to keep his mind away from it. But that didn't make any difference, I just hated him more for that. He never said anything to me about it. He never would tell me why they were getting divorced and when I asked him, he acted like he didn't understand why it was happening either. Then one day after school I went over to the hotel where he was staying. It was after he and my mom first started fighting. There was a woman there who was surprised to see me. She answered the door in a robe and said my dad was in the shower and asked who I was. I wanted to kill her. I thought I might punch her and jump on her and not stop. I said I had the wrong room and I've never spoken to him since. My mom and I moved into a small apartment and she got a second job to help pay for my college. The cancer came back a few years later and she couldn't fight it off that time."

She said it very stoically, like a hardened veteran would speak of war, calmly, without emotion, but in shambles on the inside. I talked about my father a bit afterward and was careful of how I did it because he all of a sudden looked differently in light of this new information. She was happy hearing of my family and it seemed to even soothe her.

The night breeze had turned it cool and we moved inside to the same table we sat at all together with Kevin and her friends. There was a new painting featuring a robed and haloed Jesus Christ riding a technicolored unicorn in the backdrop of the Water Land world in Super Mario Brother 3. Hadley examined the picture with a smile and laughed to herself quietly. She took a small drink from her beer glass, looked back up at the picture and then me and said, "Drew, you think, the world would be any better if unicorns were real? I don't think it would be." And then smiled, and all noise stopped for a second. It was silent everywhere; the street, the patrons, everything and everybody except for Hadley. There was a light and silent wind that blew her blonde hair around her face and she carelessly let it do what nature wanted with her. She smiled at me as though she knew everything I wanted to say and always had. Her hand went on top of mine and she became very casual like it was supposed to be there and I melted in my seat and worried she would misinterpret the sweat of my palms.

Hadley knew the world could be an ugly and cold place and she understood that human nature had made it that way. But she still loved people and didn't blame individuals and I remember thinking to myself that she could understand why I went to the war, and what I had to do once I was there. She left early and a bit drunk and I offered to walk her home, but she said that was very nice but that her roommate would come pick her up. She lived close to the bar and I wanted more than anything to walk with her for no other reason than I wanted to be with her for as long as she would let me.

"That really was such a good ending to a fucking awful day, Drew. Really, thank you so much, it really was just, exactly what I needed. I almost didn't come out too." She said

"Me either. Funny how that works sometimes." I said, wishing I had said something better.

"Yeah, it's funny sometimes."

There was hesitancy in her eyes and I could tell that she wanted me to come with her but knew it better for the both of us if it waited for another night. I wanted to kiss her before she left but reminded myself that she had just lost something close to her and that it wasn't the time for such a gesture. Twenty-two months in the most dangerous places on Earth had taught me patience as much as resilience.

I wanted more than anything to bring my lips to hers but did not. I told her how nice it was talking with her. She was still a little sad, but the beer, and I hoped me, was helping her forget it for short moments.

She came close to me and looked up and said in a wondering voice, "Why can't more people be like you, Drew Hoskins? I think maybe they think they're too busy to or something, I guess. They'll see where it gets them though."

She put on her faded blue jean jacket that came just above her hips and she pushed the sleeves up to her elbows and tugged on the inside of her lapels with angst filled frustration. I paid for her drinks and said that I would see her the next week.

"I'm pretty locked in at this point," I said.

"I hope you are, Drew," she said and put her arms around me and her head on my shoulder with her face in toward mine.

We stood in the parking lot together until her friend came. We were still hugging when she drove up and Hadley kept holding me until her friend rolled her window down and said, "Hey girl, are you feeling alright?"

Hadley brought her head up from my shoulder, and with her back facing her friend, she said to me in a soft whisper, "We don't need unicorns."

She kissed the side of my cheek, handed me a piece of paper, kissed me again, and then got in the car with her friend and I watched as she left. There was a romantic classicism to the way she did it. It was the way. I kept the piece of paper long after I put her number into my phone. I rubbed my cheek as she drove off, not thinking that she may have been looking at me from the rear-view mirror. I wouldn't have cared if she had seen anyway. There was a warmth to her lips that lingered long after they left my cheek. I didn't need to kiss hers. It was perfect the way it was. It was as Louis Armstrong said, "A kiss to build a dream on".

CHAPTER TWENTY
Zoology

IT WASN'T A DATE. At least I was trying not to think of it as a date. I wasn't sure where Hadley's heart laid, and I still wanted, more than anything else, just to be close to her. It was a Tuesday afternoon and I decided to take her to the Portland Zoo. I wanted to do something with her that I'd never done with another girl. She got very excited when I told her. She had never been to the Portland Zoo and said the one in Cleveland is small and sad feeling. I picked her up at her apartment.

Her roommate answered the door. She was quite tall, taller than me. Her hair was shoulder length and straight as an arrow, dark brown. Her eyes were prominent but not strangely big, she had a look of a young woman who knew exactly what she wanted. "I suppose you're Drew." She said as the door swung open.

"I am. How's it going?" I put my hand out. I can't say for sure that she saw it, she turned away and said, "Come in, Hadley's still getting ready. That's Hadley's room right there." The door opened right up into the living room. Hadley's roommate, whose name I didn't get, walked down the hallway, presumably to her bedroom leaving me alone to look at Hadley's closed door.

The apartment was very clean and more sparsely decorated than I had imagined. There were two bedrooms, Hadley's was the larger of the two and the one closer to the common area. The kitchen was very bright and clean and there were some sunflowers in a large simple vase on the countertop. There was a small television in the living room and a large oak-stained bookcase that reached inches from the ceiling. The carpet was the traditional apartment building tan, but they must have painted one of the walls because three were left white and one was a pale blue. I wasn't sure that Hadley knew I was there but didn't feel quite comfortable knocking on her bedroom door. For whatever reason, I also did not want to text her and say something to the effect of, 'I'm in your living room'. So I waited. I walked over to the bookshelf and was amazed to find such an assortment of books. There was everything you'd expect, a vast assortment from the canon with an emphasis on female writers like Wolfe, O'Connor, and Morrison, some Buddhist texts and over two shelves of poetry collections. But there were also many books on war, a couple on genocide and numerous on the holocaust. There were history books from nearly every country I could name and many that I couldn't. I started to panic a little. What did I know beside how to fire half a dozen weapon systems and the best way to avoid crotch rot when you can't take a shower? As I pulled from the shelf a book about a country I had never heard of called, 'Myanmar', I was surprised but not at all startled by her soft voice. "Drew, I didn't even know you were here yet."

I turned from the bookshelf and saw her more beautiful than I ever had before. She was more serene than I had imagined her or anybody capable of being. She omitted an energizing radiance that made me feel like happiness in this world was possible if you wanted it badly enough.

"I just got here, your roommate let me in, I don't know, I didn't catch her name." Shaking my head but smiling.

"Oh, god, yeah, that's Laurel, she's… yeah, you'll meet her again. Anyway, I'm so excited to go to the zoo, I live so close to it and still haven't gone."

"Yeah, it's awesome. I think you're really going to love it." I instantly regretted that statement. Why did I say love it? Why not just like? Why love? Love is way too strong. I was starting out badly, but Hadley, as she was accustomed to doing, settled my angst with her calming presence. "Oh, I'm sure I will love it. Should we go?" She said.

"Yeah, um, I drove here so we can totally drive but you are actually really close. If you wanted we could just walk there, it would only take about twenty minutes or so." I said.

"Yeah, I've gone to the Japanese Gardens up there, it's really close and it's so nice out today, let's just walk." She said.

She tried to pay for herself but let me pay without resistance when I asked. When we walked through the gate, we were so close to each other that our shoulders bumped together with every few steps. She didn't reach down and grab hold of my hand, but as we walked she would brush her hand against mine as it swayed back and forth with her gliding steps.

The first exhibit introduced us to one of the largest land predators in the world and a staple of the great Pacific Northwest, the grizzly bear. Hadley had never seen one before, and while I had, there sheer size and general magnificence was always enough to put any person in awe. There were three of them, two females and a male. Hadley asked me, "Did you ever see one of these in the wild hunting with you dad or anything?"

"No. Never even seen a black bear. I can't even imagine. Don't know if I'd have gone back in the woods again." I said.

"I bet you would have." She said while setting her hand around my elbow for a moment. The simplest touch caught my breath.

We came upon the grey wolf exhibit next which Hadley and I both especially enjoyed as dog lovers. A fact I hadn't known about her before then. She said, "I love seeing them in the wild because it makes me think about how cool it is that all dogs have that in them somewhere too. Not that they're in the wild, but you know what I mean. It's just so amazing that we've taken these animals and just bred them in all these crazy ways to get all the breeds of dogs we have now. It's just, biologically, amazing," She said.

"It really is." I said.

I wanted to buy us each a pop to drink along the way but she said that we should share one and get another one later and I was glad because it was nice to share the same drink.

I paid for two over-priced hamburgers but was happy to in the circumstance. We ate them at a table in the shade of a giant begonia tree. Its flowers were blooming dark pink and I grabbed one from the air as it fell from the tree and handed it to Hadley and smiled at her and she took it slowly from my hand and put it in her hair behind her ear and I could feel her beauty in my chest and stomach. We finished our food but sat talking for a half an hour before we got up to go to the next exhibit.

"Oh my god, look at these bats, Drew." She was eagerly three paces in front of me. It was a small, glass enclosed room full of bats. If you have never seen a bat up close before, while still a bit strange to the eye, they are a surprisingly charming little creature. They carry a lot of personality in their faces, like little dogs almost, the wings are hard to accept, not something you'd want to put your arms around or anything, but we both liked them. "I don't remember ever seen these. Must be a new exhibit or something." I said.

"These little guys are adorable. I don't know why they seem so scary." She said.

"I know, look at them, just hanging out there, doing their own thing." I said.

"You know, I think Batman is the one to blame for their shitty public image. Him and that fucking Dracula. That sucks, imagine, your whole persona ruined because some shitty comic book and the poor man's Frankenstein." She walked on to the next exhibit, holding her hand out behind her as if it were there for the taking. I rushed up to meet her and reached out for it and she grasped hold of my hand firmly and brought me to her side and we walked together in step to go look at the birds.

I wished that day would go on forever. It was perfect. Some things don't need much to be perfect, I think that's when you know that you're on to something special.

"I can't believe I never went there before. Thank you Drew. That's what I needed," she said assuredly.

"I'm glad you liked it. I hoped you wouldn't think it was stupid," I said

"Are you kidding me? That was the best time I've had since I can't even remember. I don't think I thought about anything but the animals the whole time we were here. It's nice to just think about stuff like animals sometimes."

She leaned back and smiled, and I couldn't see her whole face because of her large black-rimmed sunglasses, but I could tell that it did something very good for her.

"Yeah it is. I always loved coming here as a kid," I said.

"What was your favorite animal?" she asked.

"When I was a kid it was always the bears, but now I think I like the hippos the best. They're still really tough like the bears and stuff but they don't have to prove it by trying to huffing and puffing, you know. They just mostly get fat and float around in the water. They got things figured out I think. What did you like the best?" I asked.

"I really like the hippos too. And I really liked that giant room they had that you could walk into with all the birds everywhere. But I think I liked the monkeys the best. And not just because they're the cutest. They look like hairy little people. It's because they take care of each other so well. They bring food to their friends and clean each other's hair and you can tell they really love each other. The lions and tigers were really cool. The bears were goddamn insane, I had no idea they were that big. It's incredible seeing them so close like that, but they're so powerful and proud it's like they don't need anybody else in the world. The monkeys aren't strong or fast and don't have claws or sharp teeth or anything like that. They have to work together to keep safe. It's a lot harder to be a monkey."

CHAPTER TWENTY-ONE
Vestibule

WHATEVER BILL HAD SAID to my father must have gotten his attention. For someone who would otherwise stay silent until spoken to, he had been the first to engage in conversation with me each morning for the previous five days. I could see the concern hidden behind his eyes, and feel bad in saying that I was glad, I wanted him to know of my pain. My mother unquestioningly accepted my being home most all day and night and made me some of my favorite meals from when I was a child. They tasted at least as good as they ever had, and for that week, we felt more like a family than we had since my mom served those same meals to me twelve years before.

"Thanks Mom, this is really so good." I said.

"You still like French toast the best?" She asked.

"Oh yeah, it's still my go to." I said.

"Bill and I are going down to Carver to launch the boat if you want to go?" My father said and then took a piece of bacon from his plate, watching for my response. I was in the middle of a big bite of French toast, and made no hurry responding.

"Not today. Thanks though." I said dismissively. My father ripped the bacon in half with his teeth, chewed the first half for a moment and then put the second half in his mouth and took his empty plate to the sink.

"Why don't you go with your Dad and Bill today, Drew." My mom leaned over the table and whispered to me. I shook my head from side to side and raised my shoulders. "Drew." She said as if to repeat the same question.

"I can't go today. I'm meeting some people." I said leaned back in my chair.

"You have to meet them today?" She asked.

"Dad's coming back." I said almost loudly enough for him to hear. I sat back up in my chair and continued to eat my breakfast. My dad ate quickly but had a fresh cup of coffee, his third of the morning.

"What are you and Bill fishing for today?" My mom asked my father while looking directly at me.

"Whatever we can catch." My dad always said that when somebody asked him what he was fishing for, however, this time, the line was absent the chuckled tone he usually delivered it with to indicate it as humor. My mom reciprocated with a muted laugh.

"I mean, Dad, I would go today but…"

"No. You've got things to do, I'm sure." He said before I could finish my sentence.

"It's just that I'm meeting this gi—"

"It's fine, Drew." He interrupted.

"Maybe next time you can tell him a little bit ahead of time and he can make plans." My mother said trying to negotiate the situation the best she could.

"He knows we go every weekend. He can make plans if he wants to go." My father responded, both my parents now speaking as if I were not in the room.

"I'll go next week, Dad." I said. My mother smiled nervously.

"Okay. Just let me know in the morning if you're still going to go and I'll put your fishing gear in the back." He said.

"I'm going to go. You don't have to ask me in the morning." I said.

"Well, we'll just do it that way, so you can change your plans if you need to." He said.

"I think he wants to go next week, it sounds like he's committing now." My mom said and put her hand on my father's knee.

"Yeah, I'm definitely going to go. Count me in." I said.

My father forced a smile and raised his chin and said. "Okay. Okay then. I guess we'll see you out on the river next week then. I really hope you make it out." He couldn't just let it be. And I understood why. I had made it very hard for him. I didn't even know why anymore. I wished we had the kind of relationship where him and I would go fishing together, and I could talk about Hadley, and he could give me advice a father gives his son on such matters. And maybe we did have that kind of relationship. Maybe it was there waiting for me. I hadn't been asking the right questions. Sometimes people need you to ask them questions.

Things were going well in that Hadley and I were spending time together. They were not so great in that when we were not together, I had what felt like increasing levels of anxiety, especially late at night, alone to think about any, and all things. Luckily, I was meeting Hadley. I regretted not telling my father that she was the reason that I couldn't go right then, because I was in love with a girl who I was lucky enough to at least spend the first part of the day with. He would have understood.

Hadley wasn't reading anything that day, which was nice because I got to spend the whole time right next to her. We had our own table, centered in about the middle of the room. She was drinking a lemonade cocktail and I was drinking a beer. She had bought the first round. I had bought the second.

"That one was really good" She said.

"Yeah it was." I said.

"Sometimes I feel like I don't know the difference between good poetry and bad poetry. It's just so hard for me sometimes. If I listen to somebody's poem and it truly speaks to them, and you can see and hear than when they read it, it's hard to not think it's a good poem. I mean, if it does that for just one person, it worked. It did its job as a poem." She said and picked up her glass and brought it slowly to her lips.

"I always feel like that with your poems. I mean, not, not that they're not great, the really are, I mean anybody who really listens to them would know they're great. I mean, though how you read it, just like you said, everybody can see how much it's a part of you, your true expression. I think that's something everybody wishes they could do." I said and took a drink of my beer.

"You think I'm cool don't you, Drew Hoskins." She said as she stood up and finished her drink.

"Yeah. For sure." I said.

"Finish your beer." She said. I emptied the glass and slid it toward her and she made her way up to get us two more drinks.

It all seemed so familiar, everything we talked about, and just being there with her. It all felt like we had been doing this for years and would continue to until time ended on one of us. She was the same Hadley I had come to recognize from top to bottom. I didn't know what to account for the quick return. Was she never in love with Paul McPherson? Was he unkind to her? Was he a poor lover? He was a highway patrolman for Christ's sake, what kind of lover could he have been?

Our conversations began with simple stories of our pasts that had somehow escaped discussion on previous evenings. We talked about why I went into the army and I answered the question the best I could. I was an eighteen-year old graduating senior in high school at the time, September 11 had just happened, and I had grown up being conditioned for everything that would make a boy eager to participate in such an event. As I told Hadley why I left, I examined each word as if they were the first time they had entered my conscious, they weren't, but I'd never understood so clearly until I talked to her that day. I told her how it started when I was a kid, my mom has pictures of me holding my first rifle, a mini .22 caliber when I was just six years old, I'm wearing a woodland cammo army hat on in the picture. Scouts reinforced my interest, they even gave me little military like badges and ribbons every time I did something right. And then there was the WWII vets, we loved our WWII vets, so why wouldn't I just at the chance when my time came. It all seemed so stupid now, not going to war, but that I thought, when it was over, I'd just come home and have more stories than the guys who didn't. She asked me something else too, something nobody had ever asked.

"When did you know you were going to get out?"

"I was still in infantry school," I said after a moment.

"And what's infantry school exactly?" she asked.

"Oh yeah, sorry, you probably don't know a whole lot about the military. Sometimes I forget that people don't know the names of all these things and the acronyms and everything."

Nodding in agreement, she let a small laugh from between her lips and waited for me to continue.

"Yeah, well anyway, infantry school is where you go after basic training, if you're an infantryman," I said.

"And infantry are the ones on the ground, who do the actual fighting?" she clarified.

"Right. I think we were in something like week two of infantry school, and all the same guys in your basic training class go with you to infantry school. There is no separation for infantry recruits. So, I had been with the same guys for about three months. Anyway, I was on fireguard one night, which basically just means two guys have to stay awake and guard the barracks while everybody else sleeps, and I noticed after a while that my bunkmate, who I was on guard with, was in the bathroom for way too long. I didn't really think much of it at first, but I had to pee really bad so eventually I walked down to the opposite end of the barracks where the bathrooms were, and he wasn't anywhere around. I peed really quickly and wanted to just get back to the desk before a drill sergeant came up and saw there was nobody there, but it was just so weird. I mean, there was nowhere else for him to go, you know, I mean, it was like, where could he be, you know?"

I stopped to take a drink of my beer.

"Yeah, that must have been kind of creepy," she said.

I set my beer back down and said, "It was. Yeah, it was creepy. I didn't hear any noises or anything and all the stall doors to the toilets were wide open. I even looked in the goddamn shower, for some reason, and of course he wasn't there either."

"That's so weird."

I could tell by her expression that she did not at all anticipate the grim nature of what she was about to hear. Hesitant to go on with the story, I took another long drink.

"So, where was he, what happened?"

There was a youthful curiosity to her tone, and at that moment I decided that whatever it was I was making this girl out as was going to have to prove itself in that very moment of being real and strong like I needed her to be.

My words came quickly and without inflection, "There was a broom closet with a bunch of cleaning supplies in it. It was never shut so I knew something was wrong right away. I opened it and there he was; hanging there from a rope. He'd chewed half his tongue and his eyes had already gone gray."

Even as I was saying them, I couldn't believe the words were coming so plainly from my mouth, but she heard them, took them, and endured them. I waited for her to ask me if I were serious. That's what people always ask when they're caught off guard by something.

"Did you know him well?" she asked quickly after an initial shock that she took almost without notice. There was a slight stunt in her breath when I spoke of his chewed tongue, but that was it.

"I didn't really. He didn't talk very much at all," I answered.

"Do you still think about him?" she asked.

"No. I don't know. Kind of a lots happened since then," I said.

"I'm sorry that happened to you, Drew."

"What?" I asked.

"That you had to see that. And not just that you had to see that, but all you must have felt when it happened, and right after it happened, and even now. It's probably nothing compared to what you had to do in the war, but that alone is more than most of us ever have to deal with."

She reached her hand across the table and I met her fingertips.

My heart raced, and she said, "I guess I'm just sorry that anybody has to see those kinds of things. And it's not fair that you have to come home and see how bad it all is here too."

Every moment seemed like the right time to lean across the table and kiss her, but I wanted the moment to be absolutely perfect, and that image of perfection seemed to change with every second I spent with her. It was as though just being with her was better than the greatest book, philosophical conversation, or love making anybody could ever imagine experiencing, just sitting next to her, nothing else. More than anything, I didn't want to complicate what was already so wonderful. I think that's one of people's biggest mistakes in life, they get a hold of something good and they don't let it just be what it is, they try to get more, to squeeze more, and they ruin everything they had by doing it.

"What do you think it will take for it to all be over? Do you think it can be over?" she asked.

"I don't know. I used to think so. Now I don't know," I said.

"I want it to at least be over for you, Drew."

She put my hand in hers and looked into my eyes, but only for an instant, and I'm glad because I didn't want her to see that I was about to cry.

CHAPTER TWENTY-TWO
Paths of Glory

A FEW WEEKS AFTER school, Kevin and I finally got an apartment. My father endearingly called us morons for waiting so long and offered to help us move our stuff. None of our friends were around the day we moved so we really did need his help. I also wanted him to be there for other reasons. We hadn't done many of the things that I thought a normal father and son should do. We talked about it when we were out fishing, and he seemed excited about the plan as the day went on. And when he came, he was happy to help me and did it very enthusiastically even though he didn't miss a chance to remind us just how stupid it was waiting until after school had started to move in. Kevin was at his parents grabbing the last of his things when my dad showed up with his truck and an unusual smile. I opened the door without at first noticing what was under his arm. It was his light demeanor that caught me off guard, and when I invited him in he walked with a bounce in his step that was something like Andy Griffith had walking around Mayberry.

"I brought this for you." He said.

He held it up for me to see - the moon landing picture.

"I want you to have it for your new apartment. Put it in your room above your desk. Let it be a reminder to you."

A reminder of what he didn't say, and he didn't have to, I knew what the picture meant to him, to us.

"Thanks, Dad. Are you sure you don't just want to make a copy of it or something? I don't want to have to take this from the living room."

His expression changed as I said it and he looked almost disappointed as his still broad shoulders sunk to their sides.

Still holding the picture out for me to see, he leaned over the top of it, curiously examining it for a moment and said, "I want you to have *this* one."

I took it from him and thanked him with inadequate words and his smile returned and Kevin came back, and my dad said, "Okay you kids, let's get to work." He was as excited to help us as I'd seen him in years. He kept telling us about when he first went off to college.

"I didn't know a single person from my class who was going to U of O. I mean, I'm sure there were people who were going, but I didn't know any of them, and they didn't know me. I didn't hang out with any of those goddamn hippies or anything back then. Not even in college. My god, you should have seen all the goddamn hippies on campus when your mom and I were there. You guys won't have that anymore. I wasn't all that bad though I guess when I think about it. I don't envy you kids. That's for sure. Well anyway let's bet this couch of yours packed up in her first since it's going to take up the most room."

"Thanks so much for helping of Mr. Hoskins." Kevin said.

"Oh, it's no problem. That's what dads get to do. Just wish you knuckleheads wouldn't have waited so goddamn long."

"Well we didn't know where the best place to go was until we really got to looking." I said.

"And that's what you came up with?" My dad laughed, and I was glad that he was there and happy the way he was.

"Now grab that end of the couch, Drew and let's get this thing loaded." He said.

The three of us worked for four hours. The day was very hot. It felt good to sweat and the work we did gave a peculiar satisfaction.

I remembered the fulfillment that labor brings, regardless of the merits of the endeavor. Kevin made one last trip to his parent's, where he had also been staying, to pick up the very last of his things.

My dad and I were left alone together again. I figured he'd just leave as soon as Kevin did, but he asked me if I wanted to go to the store and he'd buy me some drinks and stuff for our new apartment. I hadn't seen my dad like that since I was a very young child and I accepted the offer and he was happy and it felt like I was a kid again riding in his big truck and running errands with him while my mom did motherly stuff at home. We talked about basketball at first.

"So, what's going on with you and this Hadley girl?" He asked.

"Were just hanging out." I said.

"And what exactly does that mean these days?" He asked.

"It means that we're not together or really dating necessarily but we're just hanging out." I said.

"So, nothing then it sounds like. I mean you guys are friends then." He said.

"Yeah, I guess so. I mean, it's more than that. I mean, the way we talk and hang out and stuff is more than just friends." I said.

"Sounds like you need to stop fooling around and tell this girl that you want to be with her. Somebody is going to if you don't. Just know that." He said. His advice was spontaneous but none the less deliberate and most of all practical.

We went into the same store we grocery shopped at when I was a kid even though it wasn't very close to where my new apartment was. I was glad he took me there. He bought me a twelve pack of cola and one of root beer and a carton of orange juice and a carton of milk.

He told me to grab myself some frozen pizzas and TV dinners and said, "When I was in college, before I married your mom, I practically lived on this stuff."

We went back to my new place and each had a pop and I smoked a cigarette outside, but only one. After the first one went out, my dad said that I shouldn't smoke another one quite yet so I didn't. We spoke for the longest I could remember since I'd stopped going on fishing trips with him in high school. The content of the conversation was unimportant at first, but it didn't matter. It's usually not what's said that really matters.

He took a verbal inventory of every tree within sight of my balcony and asked me if I knew what each one was as he pointed them out.

"That's a Canadian Maple. You know that one at least, it's a blue spruce," he said as he pointed to another. "We had one of those in the front yard until that nasty storm took it down when you were maybe five or six still."

He probably interpreted my reticence as disinterest, but I liked listening to him talk very much and wished I'd have listened to him when he told me the same stuff as a kid. He had become quiet with age though and I had grown up mistakenly equating his reservations for disappointment in his son when it was the world at large that had him so blistered. It is perhaps the greatest folly a child can commit, if to nobody but themselves, to think that a parent can ever be completely satisfied, or completely *dis*satisfied with their kid's choices. It is, however, in all our natures to contemplate, and on not too rare occasions, to dwell on where we fall on that ever-sliding scale of paternal content.

At that moment though, I felt as close to my father as I could remember and asked him, "Dad, how did you tell Mom that you loved her for the first time?"

The question made him uncomfortable, but not at all to the degree that I thought it would as I listened to the uncontemplated words coming from my mouth.

He straightened his back out, took a long sigh, leaned over the solid wood railing of my new balcony and looked over at me and said, "That's a tough one, son."

He said it not like he was talking about himself, but rather as though he knew that I was inquiring for me.

"I loved Kate, the first time I saw her, Drew. The more I was with her the more I knew it. So finally, it just happened by itself, without me having to think about it at all because it just had to come out on its own."

He was a careful but confident man and his words sounded like they came from somewhere. And I knew as he said this to me, that most of him, the good parts at least, still loved my mom like he always had.

An inconvenient phone call interrupted us, but it was an old friend that I had not talked to in a very long time and I had to answer.

As I answered, my dad silently mouthed the words, "Heading home. See you in a day or so."

I held up my finger to tell him to wait, but he kept going and closed the door behind him. I thought of saying I loved him but did not.

The phone call was from my army friend, Arthur Cantrell who I hadn't talked to since leaving the army. Cantrell was with us the night of the ambush and had lost two of his men in the fight. I didn't know what to say to him about that ever. He was one of the few soldier's whose company I missed and probably the only one who I'd have had a friendship with under other circumstances.

"Hello," I said.

"Hey buddy. What's going on?" he asked.

"Cant? Get the fuck outta here. Holy shit, dude. I can't believe it's you," I said.

"Yeah, man. How the hell are you? It's been a long time, *Hoskins*." he said.

"Yeah, dude. Way too long. Goddamn man, I can't believe it's you, man. I wanna like, go get a beer from the fridge or something," I said.

"Fuck yeah, dude. I already got one open, man," he said.

"Fuck, yeah dude, let me grab one too." I went to the fridge and opened another pop and acted as though it were a beer.

"How late is it there right now anyway, six? he asked.

"About seven," I said.

"Oh yeah, you're out there on the fucking west coast now. How is it back home anyway man? What the fuck you been up to out there?" he asked.

"It's good man. Hanging out with a couple of friends mostly. I mean you know how it is, just not the same place as when you left and shit, but hey, you know, that's all good, I'm not shook or anything. I started school and shit. It's kind of a fucking drag to tell you the truth, but I got the GI Bill money coming in every month, so I don't have to work or anything. So yeah, I guess it's all a pretty good deal really."

I wanted to tell him more but didn't know what parts would make it sound like I really was doing okay.

"You living back home with your folks?" he asked.

"Nah, man. I got a place with my one of my buddies from high school. He's going to school for his master's and knows the routine, so that's cool. Don't really hang out with too many other people though," I said.

"Lotta girls out there on the campus, I'll bet."

"Yeah, but it's not like I thought it was going to be exactly. I mean, you know, after going in the army and realizing it didn't lead to any fountain of hot, easy pussy, I figured school wouldn't resemble much of what we watched in college movies growing up. And it definitely doesn't. But I guess I did kind of still hope it would be something like that. And it is, just the thing is, I'm not really a part of any of that at all. All that kind of shit you see go down in the movies, doesn't happen unless you're in one of three or four fraternities that party with these three or four sororities. It's really all just a bunch of high school bullshit to tell you the truth, man."

But I didn't really know what I was talking about because the truth of the matter was that I never at all tried to be a part of any of that stuff and wondered why I was telling him about any of it.

"Yeah, they're not turned on about our stories about humping weight in the Ashaw Valley, or taking fire in fucking Ramadi," he said with a forced chuckle.

"Yeah, no shit man."

"Not that you really want to talk about any of that shit anyway."

I could tell he was probing. Not to be nosy or anything; he wanted to know how I was feeling about things. About where we'd been and what had happened.

"Yeah, I don't know, dude. I mean, talking to you is all good, I mean, you were there," I said hoping that it wouldn't go much further, but knowing full well that it would and that I owed it to Cantrell to talk about whatever he needed to.

"Yeah, man. I was there alright. It's really fucking good to hear from you, man."

He said it like it could easily have not been the case and I became immediately anxious in also acknowledging that possibility. Hell, it's more than a possibility. You know how people always say how in some other universe they're a rich successful person with a big house and beautiful wife or whatever? Well I bet in about every other universe it's me all fucked up and legless in a wheelchair somewhere.

"You hear about Robertson?" I asked.

"Fuck. Couldn't fucking believe it. You and him went way back," he said.

"Came to the platoon the same month. I'd been talking to him on the phone a bit." I said.

"No shit?" he said, but I didn't answer.

Not because I didn't hear him. I thought about the last conversation we had.

"You there, Hos?" he said sternly.

"Yeah, man shit, sorry. I just drifted there for a minute. It's great to fucking talk to you man. I'm sorry I didn't call you earlier. I just, I don't know. I wanted to get some time to get settled in, I guess."

"No, I get it man. You know, I could have called you too. I was going to, but I knew that you'd call me when you were ready to. But you didn't so I said fuck it and called you. But it's just good to be talking to you again, man. You know you kind of stranded me there when you left," he said, and it was true that I did.

I jumped ship right when I got the chance and I didn't look back once to look at the sinking vessel.

I didn't know what to say to that, so I just ignored it and asked him, "How's Bragg, dude?"

He paused as if unsatisfied and cleared his throat after a moment and said with his usual candor, "Good. It's good. I mean different, I'm not in the 82nd anymore. Oh shit, yeah, you don't even know any of this shit. I forget for a minute that we haven't even talked."

I again ignored the last part of what he said and excitingly responded, "What dude? You're not in the eighty-deuce anymore? You go off to fucking selection finally, man?"

"Well no, kind of, but no dude, Detachment Delta," he said.

"What, fucking Delta, you went fucking Delta?"

There was a strange panic in my voice.

"A couple months after you left man, yeah, I'm just finishing up the course," he said.

"Get the fuck outta here, man. Goddamn. Fucking Tier One. Shit, probably gonna change your fucking name and shit. I'm surprised you can even call me on the phone, man."

"Nah man, it's nothing like that. Same shit, man, just a little quicker pace and bigger targets," he said.

"Yeah, man, working with those guys along the border and up into Syria was fucking crazy. I couldn't believe some of the shit…I mean, it was fucking crazy, you know, I wouldn't shut up about all the Delta shit I got to do when you guys showed up to Ramadi. I just meant, I don't know, dude, that's just awesome I guess. Congratulations, dude. I just didn't think you were going to, you know."

My words were tripping over each other like new recruits on a road march.

"It was different once you left. I don't know, man. They called a bunch of us in for a meeting at Battalion, all E-5's and E-6's. I'm sure you would have been there if you'd have stayed in. None of us knew what it was about though. The Sergeant Major wasn't there. Not the Colonel or anybody. Nobody even from the companies, just some team leaders and squad leaders and none of us knew what the fuck was going on. A few guys were texting back to company to figure out why the fuck we were there. Then this pretty young dude who looked like he was selling boat insurance or something, came in with his gelled hair and scruffy goatee and briefcase. He went to the front of the room and put down his suitcase and opened it up facing away from all of us, so we couldn't see inside. But he never took anything out of it or anything.

We all looked at him and when everybody's eyes were on him and we all stopped talking to each other he said, "Hi fellas, I'm Master Sergeant Truman. I just want to give you guys a little briefing regarding our program here and see if any of you might be interested in coming to work for us."

That was it man, I had to see what was up. That was just a week, I think, after you left and now I'm just about done with the course. I'll go to my operation team in about a month," he said.

We spoke for the last time two weeks later. I called a month after, but the number was disconnected. His email led nowhere. No social media profiles. It was as if he had disappeared.

CHAPTER TWENTY-THREE
Utero

MY MOTHER HAD COME to Kevin and my apartment a week after we moved in. She and I met at a deli earlier for lunch. We'd never eaten there and sat outside. The air felt good because of a calm but steady breeze.

"I remember living here with your dad when we were about your age. We lived much further north, but still downtown."

"Kevin and I wanted to live close to school so we wouldn't have to worry about parking," I said.

"Yeah we didn't have to worry about that as much. The city was a lot different back then though. It was still like that when you were growing up. Seems like just in the last few years it started getting so big," she said.

"Yeah, computers, coffee, running shoes, all that stuff," I said.

"Yeah, it's too bad too. It used to be a really fun city. It still kind of is though," she said.

"Is that why you and Dad moved from downtown?" I asked.

"Partly. We wanted more room. We wanted you to have grass to run on and trees to climb," she said.

"I used to always want to live downtown whenever we came here." I said

"I remember. You always loved the city. You were so excited every time we came. Your whole face would light up and you'd be pressed against the back windows and you'd read all the signs and billboards aloud as we passed them. And you could read them all too. I think by the time you were four years old you could read them all," she said.

"I don't remember that. Reading the signs," I said.

"I sure do. Mom's don't forget things like that." The waiter was a thin, middle-aged man with a full head of long brown hair and a small mustache. He was nice. He smiled and asked if we lived in the area as he brought us our blueberry-lemonades which he recommended we ordered. We mostly people watched as we ate and after we finished I offered to pay for the sandwiches, but my mom wouldn't hear of it.

When we got to my apartment, parking was sparse, and we had to walk a couple of blocks to get there. The neighborhood was not posh. It was not poor either. It was young mostly, and maybe by proxy also poor, but not the dangerous kind of poor. My mother was not able to tell the difference. And as we passed along the way, I could see her concern.

Kevin was watching TV but turned it off and stood up as soon as we came in the door. He was always very polite like that. My mother and he hugged as they always did and she commented on how good he looked like she also always did.

I showed her around the apartment, which didn't take long because it was so small. My mother took notice. She tried her best to mask her concern, but it was obvious she had never envisioned her kin living in such a place. I thought it was nice enough. The walls were white the carpet was clean and the windows and doors all locked. And it was as good as it got for the young adult children of the middle class. This was a concept that my mother understood through her empathy for the poor, but was at the same time until then, personally disassociated from because she had grown up in the most prosperous time in American history.

"Your kitchen is pretty small, but the living room is a decent size." She said trying her best to speak positively.

"Yeah, we don't really need a big kitchen or anything." I said.

"Yeah, I guess you kids aren't going to be hosting any Christmas dinners." She said.

"No, I don't think any time soon at least. Unless we're ordering Chinese for everybody." Kevin said.

"You kids will be over for Christmas this year won't you." Her concern shifted.

"Well, yeah, I think so." I said.

"Of course, we'll be there, Mrs. Hoskins. I miss Christmas at your guys' place." Kevin said. I showed her the rest of the place and she said something strangely complimentary of each thing she saw.

"Oh, the tub is really deep. I really like that. That's really nice." She commented when I showed her the bathroom.

"You have a window next to your bed, that's good, you get good sunlight in here I'll bet." She said when I showed her the bedroom.

We were close to the school and we had a small park next to us and the rest didn't matter to Kevin or me. Perhaps for no other reason than we, unlike my parents, had to grow accustomed to the idea that the coveted business elite that were so prized by the few, were making it increasingly difficult for the rest of us to find a place to live in the city. Portland was still a strange and wonderful place, but it was getting less strange and less wonderful and the origin of its bend toward similitude was the same as that of other great metropolitans that were once celebrated for their art, diversity, and abstract city expression. The source of the dismantling, ironically, has and always will be the machine. Factory equipment had been replaced by engineering software, but it has always been the machines of the time, and their cold and calculative operators, that strip the city of its voice and its blood and its taste in the high-priced favor of almighty commerce. Portland, like any other city, was moving more and more toward becoming just another place of business. The hard-working class citizens, and the artists and writers and activists and spray painters and junkies and crazy street people that once made the city a place that the rest of the country knew as different, were pushed aside for the same bankers, lawyers, and computer geeks that turned New York from the vibrant and loud city it once was, to a sterile boring tasteless version of its former self. We wanted to think it was different out west, but the truth of the matter was whether it was LA, San Francisco, Portland, or Seattle, cash was king, and art and culture and life was only as valuable as the people with the money wanted it to be. I only mention this because it made me understand more why my mom taught math.

The living room was the largest area and was relatively big because the bedrooms were very small. Kevin sat on the green love seat my mother had purchased for us and she and I sat on the matching sofa. More than anything else in the room, my mother's eyes were drawn toward the Pink Floyd poster we had hung above our television set. The poster didn't say 'Pink Floyd' on it or anything like that. Instead, it was a giant photograph of six naked women sitting on the edge of a pool with their entire backs painted with the cover art of various Pink Floyd album covers. There was no nudity in the photograph, unless the viewer carried such conservative perspectives as to consider the uncovered back of a grown woman, nudity. My mother was no such individual and was instead greatly fascinated by the photograph and recognized one of the women to be painted in the "Dark Side of the Moon" cover.

"Oh, that's right, I know that one," she said and we all laughed together a little.

I asked her if she wanted one of the pops my dad had bought me, even though I knew she didn't drink pop.

"Oh no thanks, Dear."

And then she got up and asked where my glasses were and poured herself some water and came over with a glass of root beer with ice for both Kevin and myself.

"Kevin, so, tell me about graduate school." She said.

My mother valued education above all else, more specifically, formal education. Kevin came from a family not unlike mine, which is to say that like mine, both his mother and father had graduated college and had professional careers. While many nice houses and cars adorned the streets of my neighborhood, most came from the paychecks of light blue-collar workers that had worked their way slowly up to blending in with the middle class. My mother always regarded Kevin differently from the rest of my friends, as if we were all part of the same stock or something.

"School's good actually. A lot more reading than I had as an undergrad," he said.

"Oh yeah. I remember all the late nights and early mornings when I was going through all that. Of course, this was about a hundred and fifty years ago." She said humorously.

Whenever my mother would say something in jest, it was always self-deprecating and always had to do with either her age, or her appearance. Both of which were in better condition than she considered.

"Yeah, right, you went to Portland State too, didn't you?" Kevin asked.

My mother nodded slowly and said, "I did. I finished my Bachelors in '68 and then my Masters of Business Administration about a year and half later in '69."

My mom knew I couldn't stand it when she said *Masters of Business Administration* and smiled a playful and secretive smile and looked at me from the corner of her eye.

"So, are you going to do something in the city after this?" I interrupted.

Kevin looked at me and I ignored his curious stare and waited for my mom to answer.

"We went to eat already. We got sandwiches," I answered.

"Well we don't have to go eat. There's plenty else to do in the city besides eat," Kevin said.

"Oh, I'll probably just head home after this," my mother said.

"Well we could all go get some coffee or something," said Kevin.

"She doesn't even drink coffee." I said.

My mother drank only tea, and only at home. Kevin looked at her as if my answer didn't suffice.

"I don't, it just makes me not feel very well every time I drink it. I'll have a couple sips of Drew's dad's every now and then, but that's about all I can handle."

My mother always called my father, 'Drew's dad' when I was around.

"You can get some tea. I know a place by waterfront that has all kinds of teas. They bring them in from all over the world. China, India, Africa, everywhere." Kevin said.

"No, I'm going to head back home here soon. I'll let you boys get some of that homework done and enjoy the rest of your Saturday. You have any fun plans for tonight, Kevin?" she asked.

"I don't think I'm gonna do that much tonight. Maybe I'll meet up with this guy after he goes to his little poetry reading," Kevin said while looking over at me.

"Whatever, dude," I said back with some gasoline in my voice.

"Oh, that's right. Are you still going to those, Drew? You haven't mentioned it in a few weeks," my mother said.

"Does he still go? That's all he does every week," Kevin answered before I had the chance to say anything and I immediately became uncomfortable and wanted to leave the room.

"What's the girls name again, Drew?" she asked.

"Haley," Kevin answered.

"Hadley." I repeated slowly and looked at him with a sideways glare. "Her name is *Hadley*. Kevin's just being a dick because he wanted to go out with her friend, but she didn't like him," I added with a more mean than playful scorn.

"Drew. Don't say that. That a girl wouldn't like Kevin," my mom said.

"Well she didn't," I said.

"Drew, stop now. Listen to yourselves. Fighting about girls like you're still in high school."

Kevin paced nervously but did not look at all angry.

I boiled, and my mom turned back to me and spoke to me like she was a hostage negotiator. "Now, Drew, does this Hadley go to school?" she asked, trying to defuse the situation.

"He doesn't even know anything about her," Kevin said.

"I know plenty about her. And she finished school already for your information. She graduated last spring with *you,* in fact, *Kevin.* She went to OSU you know." I turned to my mother and said, "Besides, what does it matter if she goes to school or not?"

My agitation unfairly shifted toward her.

"Oh, I was just asking. I don't think it matters at all if she goes to school or not. Only that she's a nice person and that you like her," she said.

"Well, it doesn't matter anyway. We're not together or anything. We're just talking," I said.

"But you're writing poetry for her," Kevin said.

"Shut up!" I yelled and all the air was sucked from the room and Kevin started to say, "Sorr— "

"Just shut up, why don't you just shut up. You don't know what you're talking about!" I shouted.

"Drew jus--" my mom started to say something, but I cut her right off.

"No mom, it's fine. I got up off the couch and went into the kitchen and leaned against the counter, feeling the sweat drip from my underarms.

Kevin stood up and looked at my mom embarrassingly and said to me, "Sorry, Drew. I didn't mean anything. You know I'm only kidding. It would just be cool if you were around more, you know? Just trying to hang out before school gets too busy. I didn't mean anything. You know I really like Hadley. Tell her I say hi when you see her tonight, man."

He walked to his bedroom and shut the door, but not all the way. My mom and I went outside and we both had a cigarette on the balcony and she asked me what was wrong in the way only a mother can ask that makes you able to tell her exactly what it is.

"Mom, I love her. And I don't know how to say it. It's all I think about. I can't…I don't know what to do."

"Are you sure that you love her, Drew?"

"Completely," I said.

"Tell her then, Drew. Tell her in the purest way that you can. But make it special. She'll always remember it."

"Do you remember when Dad said it to you?" I asked.

"Of course." She said.

I waited for her to tell me the story, but she just smiled silently, and I didn't want to ruin whatever it was she was feeling.

"She makes me feel better, Mom. She's just so calming and perfect. There's no way to describe her really. Every time I try to think of how to explain her to you, I feel like I'm taking away from everything she is by putting it into words that I just don't have. I wish I could talk like she does. Then I could tell her. I wish I knew what to say to her, so she knew just how much she means to me."

"I think you need to just tell her that, Drew. Really. Any woman would want to hear that somebody felt that way about them. Because I don't think it's just that you want to tell her Drew, I think you really want her to know that you think she's that wonderful."

"I do. That is what it is. I want her to know how perfect she is. Even if she doesn't want to ever be with me, I'd still want her to know that I think that about her," I said.

"Then tell her, Drew. And tell Kevin you love him too while you're at it. He's a good friend, Drew, and not everybody is. You'll find that more and more as you get older," she said.

"I know, Mom. I will. He is. I do love Kevin. I don't know what I'd do if he hadn't moved back." I said.

"He'd probably really like to hear that," she said.

"Yeah, I'll tell him. I'll tell them both."

"You're starting to heal, Drew, but you've got to allow yourself."

"I'm trying. I want to."

"Let her help you."

"Who? Hadley?"

"Yes."

"She doesn't even know me really."

"Yes, she does. Just tell her whatever you need to."

"I don't know if I can."

"You will."

CHAPTER TWENTY-FOUR
My Heroine Hadley Landon

SHE WAS ALL THAT relieved me. We talked about books mostly at first. We could have talked about anything. Being with her was the only time worth living, and however few those times had been, they had kept me going from week to week in the desperate but patient hope that she'd let me be her salvation someday too. I felt more but I worried less. My thoughts didn't fester like dead rotting meat on the side of the hot desert road. They were more balanced. Not gone away. They were always there. The pain would always come back. But each time it was a little bit less. It stung less. It was less vivid. And the dreams were not as vicious as the time before.

There was a thickness to the air that sometimes came in the late summer days. A fragrance of flowers that I wanted to know the names of floated around us. We were sat outside for lunch at a place neither of us had been. It was a large open patio with about twelve tables and small, but healthy maple trees spread all around. The leaves were particularly green and reminded me of playing catch with my uncle because we had the same trees in our back yard. Hadley and I sat on the edge of the green patio and were next to an older couple who were loud. As always, Hadley's face captivated my attention, but there was an increasing scorn building around her eyes as the loud couple, in their late 40s I'd say, kept on. I knew Hadley was sensitive to such matters as they were making light of and wanted more than anything to keep her away from it.

"This place is kinda cool. I really dig the outdoor seating." I said.

"Yeah, I can't believe that neither of us has ever been here." She said.

"I really like your hair like that." I said.

"What, just up like this?" She asked.

"Yeah, it looks great."

"My god, no, I just threw it up really quick not really thinking about it, and then it was too late to do anything with it so I'm now just he jumbled mess sitting in front of you now." I laughed. And she smiled watching me.

"I think it looks great." I said.

"Well, that makes it easy." She said. Hadley was by this time leaned all the way back in her seat so as to better hear the couple behind her. She mouthed the words, "I can't fucking believe this" as she shook her head but with a bit of a smile. They were saying something about the war in Iraq. I couldn't hear what exactly, but it could be summed up in one sentence I heard clearly from the man who was sitting back to back with Hadley. They were the last words of the conversation before Hadley joined in. He said, "Honestly, fuck those sand niggers. We oughtta just nuke the whole fucking country."

Hadley pushed her chair back swiftly. It hit the back of the man's chair hard enough to turn him around and say, "What the fuck." But Hadley was already up and out of her seat and in front of them both at their table. I stood up and walked behind the man's chair, within arm's reach of him. "What the fuck." He repeated, sitting in his seat but facing Hadley now. His wife was silent but not nervous looking. I could see now the man was big, bigger than I was. Hadley didn't care.

"What do *you* mean, what the fuck? I fucking heard you just now. Everybody can fucking hear you. Fucking 'sand nigger', what in the actual fuck in wrong with you?"

"Hey, you don't like my conversation, don't fucking listen, I wasn't fucking talking to you." He said rather calmly.

"When you say stupid shit like that, you are talking to me. You're talking to everyone, because you're a loud asshole and we can all fucking hear you."

"Oh, whatever, fuck you, go finish your lunch with your fucking boyfriend." He said.

"I'm gonna finish my lunch asshole, but I'm going to tell you off first because what you said was bullshit and we shouldn't have to listen to that shit."

"This is America missy, don't like, don't fucking live here. Maybe you'd like it over there with the rest of those filthy mother fuckers." He said.

"Fuck you dude. Fuck you. You know what, my boyfriend fought in Iraq, fucking twice, and you're a fucking idiot." She yelled at him.

"So, he should know." He said.

"You're a piece of shit. You know that. You think you're so fucking cool with your fucking white sunglasses up on your fucking gelled hair. Fuck you dude. 'Nuke the whole fucking country'? What the fuck is wrong with you?" She started to back away a little, but the woman made that impossible.

"What the fuck do you even care honestly. If your boyfriend fought in Iraq, what the fuck do you care if we bomb them?" She asked, quite genuinely. I made my way up to Hadley who was visibly calmer but still had things to say.

"Because he told me what it was like in Iraq and I believe him." She said.

"What the hell does that mean?" She asked.

"It means that I don't think the country of Iraq deserves to have a nuclear weapon dropped on it. That's all it means. I get that some people don't understand that. I'm sorry for interrupting your lunch honestly. She took hold of my hand and I looked at the man and woman who were both saddened by the exchange and also a bit confused. I looked the man in the eyes before turning away with Hadley and shook my head slightly while locking eyes and mouthed the words 'shameful' as explicitly as I could. I put cash down on our table and we left without finishing our food.

"Let's go get a drink." She said.

"Yeah?"

"Yeah, I don't want to end the day on such a downer note." She said.

"Yeah, for sure. Let's do it. Strega?" I asked. She nodded yes, and I was glad this was happening because there was something that I had been waiting to do for a very long time. My father and mother had both told me in different ways that I needed to tell Hadley exactly the way I felt about her. Like my father had told me would happen, I had gotten to the point that my love for Hadley was bursting through every pour and could no longer be privately contained. I also dwelled on my mother's advice as to make it special when I told her, make her feel special. I didn't just want to be another buffoon professing his basic love. We drove to the bar and talked on the way there.

"Sorry about all that back there." I said.

"You? You didn't do anything. Maybe I should have just let it go or moved tables maybe. I don't know. Sometimes I just can't help it with that kind of thing." She said apologetically.

"No, not at all, don't be sorry at all. I thought it was great honestly. I mean, I obviously wish none of that would have happened in the first place, but it was crazy seeing you like that, anybody like that, willing to just say something to a complete stranger like that. But we should be doing stuff like that, all of us." I said.

"You don't think I'm weird or anything." She asked

"No. I think it's weird that we don't all do that kind of thing all the time. That's what's weird." I said.

We arrived at Strega in time to catch a couple readings. Hadley and I were as close as we'd been. We held hands side by side with our arms interlocked like it was the first time either of us had had somebody to hold. I felt warm and at home and realized that was the feeling of true love. Being with that person, next to them is all you need to rest and know all that really matters is being able to keep coming back to that place that rests the demons.

"I love being here with you, Drew. I'm so glad you came in here that day. I can't imagine what I'd still be doing right now. Where my head would be." She kissed me, and I kissed her back and put my hands on her warm cheeks and knew that it was time.

"I have to do something." I said to her.

The stage was empty, but the microphone stayed on and standing. Reaching into my pocket, Hadley stood looking up at me with her hands interlocked and up toward her chin.

I looked into her eyes and wanted to mouth the words, 'I love you', but instead, I pulled the microphone from the stand and said, "I wrote this thinking about you" and began reading the only poem I've ever shared.

Bits of broken glass speckle the night sky
I sit and wait for her to fall from the moon again
The surface is dry and white
But for a patch with green lush trees
I eat the figs that she plucks from the trees that grow in the spring each year
I won't see her when she comes this time
Another form is filled and felt and out of the dim light she curls and bends
Weightless and gossamer, the face of a thousand whispered voices cools my ear
and bends my spine and the moss is wet and I can hear as the serpent crosses
the covered roots
Does she watch me trace the sleeping dew?
I heard your breath and you swallowed mine,
and we were one and whole
before we drifted out to sea and apart again.
May the wind pluck at my shape
And carry me away into the ether
Someday you'll be in that moon again
And you'll find me there waiting

It was a terrible poem, and I knew this more than ever when reading it aloud. But it was not to her. She cried and smiled. and the tears kept coming down from her face and she got up on the stage and she kissed me and people clapped around us, not for my poem, but for us, for love, they all knew what they saw to be true. It was the purest love I had ever felt and the only version worth remembering. She looked at me and my face was wet with her tears and she said to me, "I love you Drew. I love you so much." And I knew that my life would be fine, if that were all I ever had, if it all ended right then and there, it would be just fine.

Sunrays peaked through the thin blinds as an introduction to things to come. I felt the warmth across my chest. The blankets were down around my stomach and the morning was warm and bright and seeped through my thin drapes because the blinds were left open from the day before. I could smell her scent on the pillow and held it to my face and breathed in deeply and my heart slowed with a calming beat and things felt safe.

It sat on my desk as if it were the only thing that ever really existed on the face of the earth. It was all that mattered, and its words held all the answers to this life and everyone to come. The paper was folded into thirds and propped up in a triangle with my name written on the outside and facing parallel to where I was in bed. I threw off the blankets and got up nakedly and desperately and held the paper in my hand tightly between my thumb and forefinger before opening it. It was written in fine black ink and the heading said, 'had to go to work.' Underneath it read:

Sleet and rain turned to stark dying dryness. I dragged my heavy heart across the earth. Every land was different but always with the same loneliness. I looked to God for comfort, but he was infinitely occupied. The thick sickness had been with me for many lifetimes. Desolation and darkness had been my companion for all of them. I came to the edge and looked down, my toes hung over just slightly. Time was interrupted by the incomprehensible gentleness I felt as your hand grasped mine. I didn't need to turn and look, I knew it was you. It would always be you. Our bodies began to fade away as our souls took their places. And we continued forward.

As I read her freshly penned words, the world I had created from my watchtower had come true. It wasn't the same one I talked about perhaps, or even ever imagined. It was better, it was perfect, it was real salvation. I was useless to existence and at the same time the most powerful being that had ever lived. I knew nothing anymore but was filled with the only piece of knowledge that I'd ever need again. I became aware of the utter insignificance of all things peripheral to Hadley Landon.

The war was still there for me. It was still there for all the other men and women still fighting and dying and coming home and salvaging whatever they could. But I found what I needed the day I walked into that bar and saw my salvation living triumphant onstage.

Dumbstruck and dug in with toes buried into the carpet of my bedroom floor, my heart raced, and I had to sit on the bed's edge. All feeling dropped to my stomach and beat deep down and felt strangely good.

At the bottom of the note was a lipstick outline of her delicate mouth. I traced the edge with my fingertip and pressed the painted lips to mine and could smell her on the paper. My sweet Hadley, who I'd found by complete accident, or what had seemed like an accident, was looking for the same thing.

She hadn't been to where I was and she hadn't done what I had, but the world had shown her its darker side like it shows us all in its own harsh way. Everything beautiful about the world came together all at once and showed itself to me in a way it never had before.

For a short time, there was no more sickness or sadness or death or rot. It all shined and was wonderful in the greatest month the Earth had ever felt. It was Monet, it was Beethoven, it was a Shakespearean sonnet and all the brightest and best things about life—pure and isolated and as new and alive. I heard my chorus and knew it for the first time as love.

The days are still rough and nights long and too often sweaty, but I can at least look back on it all now and know that however terrible it might have been, it's what put me in the saving embrace of the only god I've ever known. Alive and relentless as my war might rage on, in the end, she will be what deepest remains.

ABOUT THE AUTHOR

Photo credit: Shannon Balazs

Joseph Andrew Holsworth is the author of the autobiographical war novel, *The Devils of Eden* and his most recent work, *What Deepest Remains: the journey home..* He was born and raised in the Pacific Northwest. After serving four years and three tours as an infantryman with the 82nd Airborne Division, he graduated from the University of Nevada with a degree in literature before moving to Berkeley, California with his wife. He taught public school in Oakland before dedicating himself completely to writing.